THE ART
OF
JAPANESE PAPER

THE ART
OF
JAPANESE PAPER

MASKS
LANTERNS
KITES
DOLLS
ORIGAMI

DOMINIQUE
BUISSON

TERRAIL

Cover
illustration:
Lantern craftsman

*The lantern craftsman
must be an excellent
painter and a
calligraphist with a
steady hand.*

Preceding page:

*The inside of a
Jingasa from the Edo
era made of lacquered
paper and decorated
with gold.*

Editors: Jean-Claude Dubost and Jean-François Gonthier
Art director: Bernard Girodroux
Translation: Elizabeth MacDonald
in association with First Edition Translations Ltd, Cambridge.
Composition: Artegrafica, Paris
Filmsetting: Compo Rive Gauche, Paris
Lithography: Zincografica Fiorentina, Florence

© FINEST S.A./ÉDITIONS PIERRE TERRAIL, PARIS 1992
ISBN: 2-87939-009-5
Printed in Italy

Contents

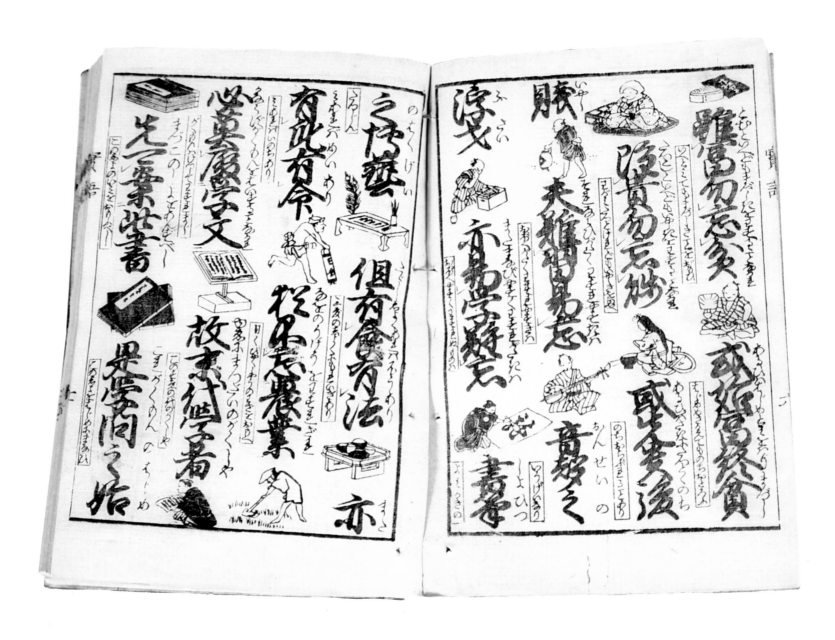

**Book from
the *Edo* period**

*Book depicting minor
crafts greatly in vogue
in the Edo period.*

A paper culture

Throughout time, paper has been the mirror of the soul.

Exceptional in its suppleness, solidity and whiteness, yet easily destroyed, this material has shown itself to be so entirely "human" in its weaknesses and faults that it has become the symbol of culture itself. Without it, there would be no history, no memory. It has passed on divine wisdom, philosophical precepts, scientific laws and political will. Writers, historians, poets and painters all owe their livelihood and their public recognition to paper.

From its very beginnings, paper has expressed mankind's highest quality – that of nobility. In comparison to paper, materials such as sculpted stone, engraved wax, carved bamboo and decorated parchment all seem too crude to record the memories of civilisation. Even though silk, that incomparable material, has sometimes lured away poets and painters, paper nonetheless maintains its privileged role as friend of the spirit.

Japanese paper, called *washi*, is not only used to carry writing. By virtue of its purity, it is also a symbol of sacrifice and of respect for the gods and for man himself. Folded or cut out, it extends the scope of speech and gesture. Although it emphasizes the Ideal and the Beautiful, it can also be functional when used as clothing, wrapping material or the basis of a plaything. Consequently the craftsman who fashions it awakens the spirit to the sensuality of touch, to the delicacy of the sense of smell and to visual nuances.

This unmatched richness of the senses led the West to believe that the bloodthirsty warriors of the Japanese archipelago had forgotten their harsh destiny in the tranquillity of their "house of paper", weeping into their brocade sleeves while reading a poem about the fall of a cherry

Young woman reading

7

Scene from the *No* theatre

Scene representing a demon spider casting its web over a valiant warrior. The threads of the web are ribbons of paper hidden in the actor's sleeve.

blossom petal. It was tempting to imagine them sitting next to a gold leaf parasol or a lantern decorated with calligraphy, waving a fan while contemplating a print or the flight of a kite. This rather excessive exoticism shows that the West favoured a certain image of Japan in which paper was the cultural symbol, and this is not entirely false, if one considers that the cultural level of a country is measured in particular by its paper consumption.

At the dawn of its modernity Japan certainly lagged behind Europe, but its compulsive consumption of paper vouched for its high standard of education, art and craftsmanship. At that time, Japan produced more paper than any other country in the world and had based a whole civilisation on its use. Paper formed a part of every aspect of daily life. Illustrated books cost "no more than a bowl of noodles" and the memories of an entire nation were accessible to everyone. This explains the incredibly low level of illiteracy in 1890: 2% among boys, 5% among girls.

Since the very beginning of its history, this idea of education by paper has been firmly rooted in the mentality of the Japanese people. Before it becomes a permanent record of words, forms and images, paper is virgin and rich in promise. While Westerners refer to paper manufacture, the Japanese speak of *kami-suki*. This term, which implies the idea of the cultivation of beauty, could be translated as "rearing paper" or "paper education". Perhaps we can see in this the direct complicity of paper and the original Japanese religion, *shinto*.

Many paper-related arts received support and often their inspiration from *shinto*. As a result, the craftsman who has the task of "rearing" such noble material must be sincere, honest and pure in his work, since the slightest taint of darkness in his spirit will transfer itself irrevocably to his paper. He must also exert physical effort and undergo physical suffering, because if paper demands love, it also calls for snow and sun, cold weather and icy water. Yet even this is not enough, for each stage in the manufacture of paper requires unwavering attention: from harvesting the plant fibres to drying the paper sheets, the smallest error of choice, the merest delay in treatment, the slightest lapse of supervision would be fatal to the paper. This is the uncompromising domain of excellence.

For all these reasons, the use of natural handmade paper always betokens respect. Once it was a gift as rare and precious as a piece of lacquerware or a roll of silk.

Its whiteness even took on a cosmic meaning, since it evoked purity, and thus the innocence of birth, as well as mourning. In time it acquired so many different uses that by the 18th century there were over one hundred varieties of paper, each corresponding to a particular occasion. With the opening up of Japan to the West at the end of the 19th century, Japanese paper became internationally renowned. Its quality of extreme solidity and the nobility of its manufacture made it the ideal medium with which to immortalise the great moments of history. It was thus chosen over its

Poster

*"Paper" exhibition at
the Meguro Art
Museum in Tokyo.
Folded shapes by Koji
Tashiro.*

only rival, Kent paper, for recording the articles of the Treaty of Versailles on 28th June, 1919. It is still indispensable for making five lead print copies in art publishing. Numerous artists, including Rembrandt, used it for sketching the outlines of their masterpieces.

Paper, the medium of expression, is itself expressive through its texture and the immense variety of treatments it can undergo. Its world renown is due to the incredible quality of its fibres, though Westerners credited it with less than modest origins by baptising it "rice paper". They thought its fibres came from rice straw, or that the grain itself was used in its manufacture. Although Japanese craftsmen did on occasion add rice powder to paper pulp to reinforce its whiteness, and although rice straws or husks were sometimes used to make low-grade paper, these techniques were not generally used. During the course of its history, many plants were tested to see if they could perfect the texture of Japanese paper, but it was three in particular, *gampi*, *kozo* and *mitsumata*, that gave it its originality.

According to Yanagi Soetsu, an authority on traditional arts, these three materials were the true basis of Japanese papers.

Paper made with *gampi* is the best quality and the most durable. Both soft and strong, it is glossy, non-absorbent and unaffected by humidity: it is the paper equivalent of silk.

Kozo (mulberry) paper is masculine. Its long, thick, solid and sinuous fibres can withstand the toughest treatment. Its texture can vary, its surface can be uneven, porous and malleable: it is the equivalent of linen.

Mitsumata paper is feminine. It has softness, grace, chastity and elegance. Its soft and modest texture gives it a slightly lustrous charm: it is the equivalent of cotton.

Waxed, crumpled, rubbed, modelled, twisted, shaped, torn, folded, perforated, lacquered, oiled, waterproofed, woven, glued or sculpted, Japanese paper can replace many other materials – cloth, rope, straw, leather, bamboo, wood or glass. Or it can finish them off to perfection to make marvellous parasols, fans, lanterns or boxes. The list is long, but the destiny of Japanese paper is worth following, and we should take note of a branch of knowledge which is all too often ignored in the rest of the world.

Amid today's world of concrete and computers, Japanese paper remains a privileged testimony to the richness of the Japanese soul. Though its future cannot be predicted, one thing is certain: difficult to create and easy to burn, it will always be reborn from its ashes.

**Detail of a New
Year decoration**

*The fan is a symbol of
prosperity as it expands
progressively.*

**Traditional
painting**

*Painting depicting two
noblemen on a
veranda, from the
Momoyama period.
This painting adorned
a study-library corner
in a traditional home.*

A short history of paper

The exemplary life of Ts'ai Lung
in the workshops of the Celestial Empire

Nothing apparently predisposed the young Ching Hung to a place in history. He was born in China, far from the Imperial capital in the province now known as Yunan, where modest living conditions ensured that people lived out their lives quietly and did not as a rule become famous. This region was very important to the central government of the Chinese Empire, however, as it possessed iron, copper and zinc in abundance. So the young man from the provinces, who as an adult took the name of Ts'ai Lung, was recruited as a foundry worker in the capital. The chronicles tell little of his life – we know hardly anything about his development until he was appointed chamberlain to the imperial family in 75 ad. From then on, his destiny was to be exceptional.

The Emperor Chang died two years later, bringing to power a ten-year-old Emperor Ho, with whose political education Ts'ai Lung was entrusted. The dowager Empress T'ou tried to seize power, aided by her brother Hsien. The upright Ts'ai Lung protected the interests of his imperial pupil and helped to oust the usurpers. In recognition, the Emperor Ho appointed him head of the Imperial Workshops, an elevated position which allowed him to compile a register of all the techniques practised in the empire and to participate in some, such as the manufacture of sabres. One of his tasks was to supervise the upkeep of the imperial Library, to which the emperor attached great importance. It was thus that he discovered the art and methods of writing used in China.

Papier-mâché object

Embossed paper purse and coins from the Edo period. Today, Japanese banknotes are still some of the most robust in the world. Their origin goes back to the Echizen clan at the beginning of the Middle Ages. At the start of the 18th century, 244 clans were producing their own coinage until a national Minister of Finance was created in 1868.

Opposite:
Polychromatic print

Print from the Edo period depicting a geisha procession. The parasols are embossed with the coat of arms of their house.

The invention of paper

One of man's first aims was to find a means of preserving the fruits of his fertile imagination. Bone, ivory, skin, clay, metal, bark, stone, palm leaves, waxed wood, silk and papyrus all accompanied the first steps in writing. In the library, Ts'ai Lung discovered many examples of writing media, along with numerous texts describing their use. At that time, China was making great use of carved strips of bamboo, which occupied considerable space on the bookshelves and required thousands of hours of classification and restoration. Silk was also used for the most important writings, but it was rare and expensive to make. Amongst all the silk and bamboo, the master of the Imperial Workshops discovered that craftsmen had been attempting to perfect a revolutionary writing medium. Although very much cheaper and far less bulky, this product was still far from perfect. Its improvement was a problem on which Ts'ai Lung worked unrelentingly for several years. He made the "pulp" from macerated silk flock drained on a sieve, which when dried made sheets that could be written on. He then experimented with complementary fibres such as linen, hemp, bamboo, laurel, reed and even Chinese herbs, using them singly or in combination. Ts'ai Lung conducted this research at a time when he was no more than a lesser imperial servant. The appearance of the word "paper" in the first Chinese dictionary published in 69 ad bears witness to this development. Ts'ai Lung's achievement was to promote the production of a more effective paper, made essentially of long-fibred vegetable material. This was reduced to a watery pulp and filtered through a sieve. Its dried residue made a sheet which could be written on. The ingredients for the pulp were old macerated fishing nets, worn hemp, rags of various kinds, and most importantly tree bark. He finally chose the bark of the mulberry tree, beaten and separated into thin fibres to which he added a mucilagenous substance to glue them together.

Modern paper thus came into being.

Ts'ai Lung promoted it and introduced it at court. From that time on he became the official "inventor" of this unrivalled product, the source of our memory.

All this took place in 105 ad.

Prince Shotoku, in the steps of Buddha

A Japanese chronicle called the Nihon Shoki tells us that the technique of paper making was introduced into Japan five centuries later in 610 by the Korean doctor and priest Tam-Chi (*Donchô* in Japanese). Korean monks had introduced the mysteries of Buddhism to Japan fifty years before along with its architecture, statuary and sacred texts. These texts revolutionised Japanese culture: from this time onwards, writing and its perfect medium, paper, became a necessity.

In 610, the Prince Regent Shotoku had been in power for seventeen years. Shrewd and entrepreneurial, he was also gifted with great aesthetic sense. He found Chinese paper fragile and brittle, which detracted from its noble function. He therefore undertook to improve its texture, and encouraged the planting of mulberry and hemp throughout the country. These two materials were already cultivated to make clothing, and the Prince's intervention also spurred on the production of silk in Japan. Almost immediately, the technique was discovered of boiling fibres mixed with a solution of wood ash, and of adding to them a glutinous vegetable substance. From this time on, Japanese paper, with its characterics of solidity and elegance, proved itself to be more effective than its Chinese model.

The Nara period (710-794) – the golden age

Under the aegis of Buddhist monks, all the refinements of Chinese culture penetrated Japan. Arts and industry were developed with enthusiasm, and gradually paper-making spread to the provinces. During this period, hemp was the basic material in use: the bark of the mulberry and the *gampi*, a similar plant, would follow later. Two fundamental elements simultaneously brought about the birth of authentic Japanese paper: the technique of *nagashi-zuki* (the art of making the pulp "run" over the sieve) and the discovery of the mucilaginous qualities of the *tororo-aoi*, an aquatic plant. Instead of merely being useful, paper could now become a work of art.

Up to 180 different kinds of paper were used in official Nara documents. Some of these are dyed bright red, indigo, green, yellow and blue. These variations had as their main purpose the honouring of Buddha and

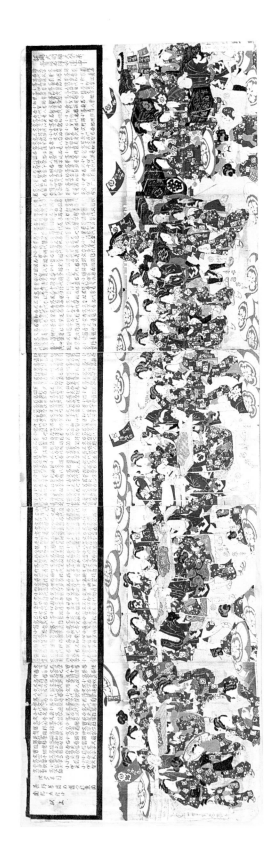

Firemen's totemic ensigns

These objects identified the different squads of firemen arriving at the scene of a blaze. In time, they became symbols of rivalry between the factions, which sometimes fought among themselves for the honour of extinguishing a fire.

Opposite:
Account book belonging to a trader from the *Edo* period

The pages were generally made of waterproofed paper.

the recording of sacred words. Copying these texts became fashionable among aristocrats, to the extent that an office was set up at court specifically for this purpose. As a result, the demand for paper escalated. At the end of the period, twenty-three chosen regions were producing thousands of sheets of paper per year, the majority of which was sent as tax to the capital.

In 770, paper-making techniques were sufficiently advanced to carry out Emperor Shotoku's great plan for ensuring peace. This involved printing a million Buddhist charms from wooden blocks. Each sheet of paper, measuring 6 x 45 cm, was placed in a small wooden pagoda before being consecrated in one of the capital's ten temples. They are the oldest known example of printing.

The Heian era (794-1192) – the aristocracy of paper

The Emperor Kammu transferred his imperial residence to Heian (now known as Kyoto) to escape the increasing influence of Buddhism and the absolute power of its monks. Under the exclusive control of the aristocracy, a particularly refined culture came into being. Japanese craftsmen became attuned to the effete, poetic mood of the imperial court; paper became its ideal reflection.

Paper-making technology was now unequalled. Hemp was abandoned in favour of mulberry in the production of a large number of provincial varieties, and these were much used by the nobles and clergy. In 807, the government created the imperial Kanya-in (or Kamiya-in) mill on the banks of the river Kanya. The best craftsmen were recruited to perfect the art of *shikishi*, or the "pretty leaf". They wasted no time in bringing into general use the technique of "floating the fibres", to replace that of "still water on the sieve". This new method, which today is still confined to Japan, allows large sheets of paper (60 x 36 cm) to be produced with an even distribution of pulp. The imperial mill was not alone in producing high quality paper. The northern provinces in particular were soon proud to be producing better paper than the capital. Paper from Mutsu (in the Aomori prefecture) was in fashion for decades. In 930, Ki No Tsurayuki, a nobleman and the author of the famous *Tosa Journal*, was

**Court dance using
a fan**

*The hat is made of
oiled paper.*

sent to Tosa to assume the duties of governor. For five years, he devoted himself to the development of this poor and forgotten region. Establishing paper production was one of his priorities. He accomplished this to such an extent that the high quality paper from this region was used for the imperial documents and official memoranda of the 10th century. At the end of this period, the Kanya mill went into decline and specialised in recycled paper.

The elevated life-style of the Heian aristocracy encouraged the blossoming of the most extreme nuances in all fields, and in particular in the area of personal feelings. This is the period in which literature first appeared. Women excelled in the courtly novel and in bedside notes, and their admirers made it a duty to know how to write verse. The privileged intermediary between these lovelorn souls was, of course, paper, which expressed their sentiments well. At the end of the 10th century, the noble lady Sei Shonagon confided:

"Even though the world is wearisome and I want to flee from it, when I am given beautiful white paper all is well."

Following in the tradition of calligraphy, paper expresses itself in nuances. Its names vary according to its use or the type of writing it bears. Sheets of paper intended for calligraphy can simply be dyed, but the most striking are those which have collages of variously treated papers, or skilful mixtures of pulp, or those that include flowers or fabrics. Thus the poet's art consists in following the rhythms of the paper. It is no surprise that perfumed paper also made an appearance.

The Japanese Middle Ages (1192-1603) – the paper of warriors

The naval battle of Dan-no-ura in 1185 sounded the death knell of the imperial aristocracy. From that moment on until 1868, Japan's destiny was in the hands of the military. At the start of this long period, a spirit of austerity dominated the cultural life of the warriors, in contrast to the decadent refinement of the imperial court, which was stripped of all power. A taste for plain, simple, humble paper became widespread, in line with a striving for a certain ascetism, which was being promoted by the newly established Zen Buddhist sect. This did not last for long. The splendours of the capital soon haunted the dreams of the *shogun*, who quickly returned and settled there. The 15th and 16th centuries were as fertile in stylistic affectation and riches as they were in wars.

Paper benefited from this troubled time. The clans were rivals not only in arms but also in the quality of the products from their own fiefdoms. However, feudal laws tried to ensure a certain standardisation of production in the country. The systematisation of currency in the 14th century gave rise to the foundation of commercial guilds, and thus to a better distribution of consumer goods, with some centres specialising in certain crafts. At the close of the 16th century, paper was sold in the markets of Kyoto and was even exported to China and Korea. Not far from the capital, the village of Mino devoted all its energy to the production of *Mino-gami*, the name of which soon became synonymous with "paper". Around the paper-making vats, the makers of parasols, lanterns and fans set up their business, and these items are still products of the region today. However, paper remained an expensive item in many provinces. The geography of Japan, the clan wars and poor transport made paper a rare material, and one which people considered a tasteful gift. Among the most popular presents was "sparrow" paper, which was created in the province of Echizen and was speckled like a quail's egg. Another popular present was paper made from the fibres of a new plant, the *mitsumata*. The discovery of this plant was of great help, as it could be cultivated like the mulberry, while *gampi*, which only grows wild, was becoming increasingly hard to find.

The Edo era (1603-1868) - the universality of paper

The *shogun* Tokugawa Ieyasu imposed a permanent peace on the 66 Japanese provinces. For two and a half centuries, the Tokugawa clan ruled the country from its capital, Edo (today's Tokyo). Fiefdoms were redistributed and any warlike inclinations were stifled. Overlords were forced to develop their resources, and paper and lacquerware were ranked second and third behind rice as sources of taxation. Each clan had its own manufacturing secrets, but espionage enabled tech-

Paper flowers

The art of making paper flowers goes back to the 8th century. A collection of poems from this century describes making a sheet of typically Japanese paper for the first time. In the Heian period, these flowers became an indispensable part of the decoration of Buddhist altars. Paper was also used when transporting real flowers for ikebana bouquets. Such wrapping consisted of an envelope of oiled paper, with ties, sometimes still used by traditional masters.

Tosa paper

Tosa paper was often chosen for the restoration of famous temples. In 1925, sheets of paper 2.7 metres wide were designed to replace the partitions of the Kinkaku-ji temple in Kyoto. The frame was supported by three people. In 1936, sheets of paper of the same size were made for the Meiji-jingu shrine in Tokyo. Only one person was needed to manipulate the frame.

niques to spread and improve throughout Japan. Three production centres dominated the market: Gifu, where *Mino-gami* was so popular that its sheet size became the standard size for books; Kochi, whose *Tosa-washi* represented 40% of the paper handled by Osaka merchants; and Ogawa, 80 km from Edo, which supplied a local population of 1,300,000 with paper.

The Edo period was particularly rich in the creations of craftsmen. Japan, cut off from the world on the whim of its rulers, had no recourse other than to improve its art of living. Japan's passion for natural materials, its taste for ritual and its veneration of skill urged the Japanese craftsman strive constantly after quality, even in the production of the most ordinary everyday objects.

The immense variety which we see in the use of paper at this time is the most obvious proof of this.

Two innovations are typical of this period. Shizuoka's *suruga-hanshi* represented the first real attempt to standardise paper. These were half-sheets measuring 25 x 35 cm, perfect for the manufacture of parasols or paper partitions. Westerners were particularly intrigued by *yoshino-gami*. Its texture was so fine that it was not only used to filter oil or lacquer, but also as toilet paper. Later it was exported to the USA for the manufacture of coffee filters. Genda Yoshii (1826-1908) from Tosa created a "demi-format in *mitsumata*", which was only equalled by his *tengucho-shi*, the paper with the finest texture in the world. This inventive craftsman improved the tools of his art at the same time, and is considered to have established the basis for the modern paper industry.

The imperial restoration of the Meiji in 1868 had the effect of opening up Japan to the West. The temptations of modernity soon prevailed over the preservation of old values. In 1798, the paper making machine was invented in France, and this was one of the first importations of European technology. The first Japanese industrial mill was founded in 1873 by Eiichi Shibusawa. Rivalling the Western factories established in Yokohama, it was called Japan's Oji Paper Company, and was situated in the northern outskirts of Tokyo. Traditional paper resisted the new industrialisation, but could not contend for long against it and the need for modern paper in the early years of the 20th century. *Washi*, or "Japanese paper", had no *raison d'être* in a now "modern" nation.

Today *washi* once more fulfils a cultural need. Unfortunately most of the production centres had lost their know-how, and it wasn't until the rediscovery of Japanese "folk-crafts" by isolated artist-craftsmen and by some admiring Westerners that Japanese paper was reborn from its ashes. It is organised today under government auspices around the three towns where this new "industry" has grown up: Goka, in the prefecture of Fukui, Makidani, in the prefecture of Gifu, and Ino, in the prefecture of Kochi. In the latter, Tosa *tengucho-shi* has been classified as "cultural property" like many former regional creations.

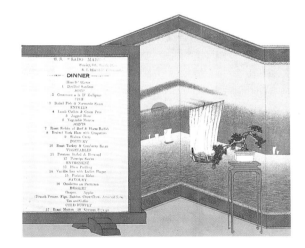

Menu from a Japanese steamship, 1910

These menus for Westerners were frequently decorated in the Japanese tradition, but were printed on Western paper.

The making of washi

Paper-making is regulated first and foremost by the rhythms of country life. Farmers only undertake the production of paper when the harvest is over and silk has been spun. The working season varies from region to region, but is generally at the end of November or beginning of December. The production of paper requires two essential conditions: cold weather and very pure water, so mountainous areas are the most suitable. However, the presence of damp during its manufacture ruins paper. The majority of paper mills are therefore on the Pacific coast of Japan, where winters are drier. In spite of the excellent climatic conditions, the craftsman is not sheltered from sudden rain, snowfalls or unforeseen frosts. The art of paper-making always has an urgency about it.

Water, present at all stages of manufacture, must be pure, cold and fast flowing. Areas with paper mills are always close to water low in iron and manganese, since these metals are damaging to paper. In these fast-flowing waters, coolness and movement considerably limit the growth of bacteria, ensuring the paper's durability.

Cold is equally vital, to strengthen and contract the fibres of this living material, and give it a solid, fresh and firm appearance. Paper made in the summer always seems limp and indifferent.

Plants used for paper

In addition to water and cold, the basic materials consist of vegetable fibres which give *washi* its special

Opposite:
Gampi

One of Japan's native plants used to make its traditional paper.

From fibre to paper

Opposite:
Kozo "black skins"

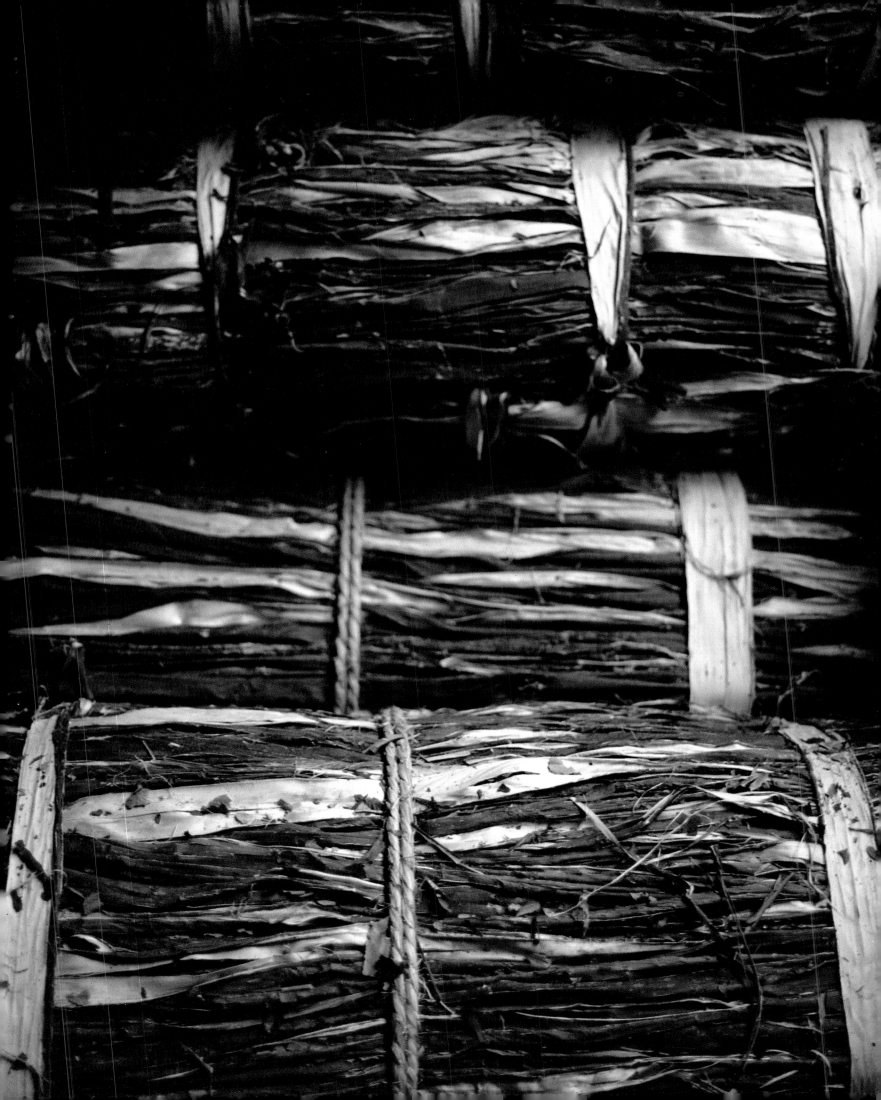

Twists of bleached fibre

Opposite:
Thin, transparent paper

This type of paper is used for wrapping or for decoration. This sheet of paper contains inclusions of gold leaf.

characteristics. Among these fibres are those of the *kozo* (*broussonetia kajinoki*), *gampi* (*diplomorpha sikokiana*) and *mitsumata* (*edgeworthia papyrifera*). The most frequently used plant is *kozo*, followed by *mitsumata*. *Gampi*, which only grows in the wild, has become very rare.

Kozo, gampi and mitsumata

The *kozo* belongs to the same family as the mulberry (used for breeding silkworms) and it usually grows in the same fields.

Several varieties of small shrub lay claim to the name *kozo*. *Kajinoki*, which grows in the Northern regions, is native to Japan and is without doubt the best. In second place is *broussonetia papyrifera*, a native of the Asian continent, which has longer fibres than the former. *Tsurukozo* only grows on the island of Kyushu and is virtually extinct.

Kozo is planted in the spring on south-facing slopes. It needs to grow for at least two years before it can provide fibres which are suitable for paper. The twigs are harvested in Autumn, as soon as the leaves have fallen, which is the time when the bark is best, or in February or March. They are cut to about a metre in length and tied into bundles to be heated or "cooked".

The seven or eight varieties of *gampi* are collected from February to May when the branches are still saturated with water. They are then stripped of bark without prior seasoning and are dried. Their long, fine fibres are totally resistant to insect damage.

Mitsumata belongs to the same family as *gampi*. Its name derives from the division (*mata*) of its branches into three (*mitsu*) at each node. Planting is in June, with the saplings being protected from the wind by young cedars or cypresses. Harvesting is in December and March. *Mitsumata* grows mainly on the island of Shikoku in the Tosa region, near Mount Fuji and on the Izu peninsula, where it was discovered at the end of the 15th century. Its spongy fibres are shorter than those of *kozo* or *mitsumata*. It is more often used in combination with the latter two and is by far the easiest to work with. Its suppleness and resistance to insects made it the choice for the manufacture of banknotes.

Decorative paper

The Japanese are very sensitive to the beauty of the visible fibres which are a feature of their paper. Reflections on water, or clouds, these material patterns evoke deep emotion.

Tororo-aoi and nori-utsugi

The term *neri* (or *nori*) is generally used for all mucilaginous substances which keep the fibres in suspension in the pulp tank. Once the pulp is removed, these substances prevent sheets from sticking together when stacked, thus dispensing with the need for the intermediate felt used in the pressing of Western paper. Thanks to this viscous decoction, we still find very ancient paper which has withstood the ravages of bad weather and humidity. People were even advised to throw important documents into water tanks in the event of fire. These would then be retrieved completely separate from each other. This would not be the case with Western paper, since it contains a large proportion of glue to hold its fibres together. This substance also enables strong sheets of paper to be made, as fine and transparent as a veil.

Tororo-aoi is the most frequently used mucilage. It is sown just before the rice is planted, cut in July to improve the roots and harvested in November. *Nori-utsugi* grows mainly in Hokkaido. The substance is extracted from its inner bark which is quite thick, since the shrub takes many years to grow.

To make good paper, the quantities of *tororo-aoi*, water and pulp must be measured out accurately. Everything depends on the quality of the paper sought, its thickness, the season and the climate. It is estimated that about fifteen years' experience is needed to master this stage of paper-making.

Paper making

The process does not differ radically with the plant in use. The shrub is stripped of its bark and its fibres are separated, cleaned in an alkaline bath, bleached and beaten. The resulting pulp is then taken out and cut into sheets. These are stacked, drained, dried and graded.

The technique for making *gampi*-based paper is a good example of this process.

The saplings are harvested, stripped of their bark and dried, before being tied into bundles of "black skins".

With *kozo* and *mitsumata* the stems are seasoned before the bark is stripped. Women do this work, splitting the bark with their nails and removing it from the wood, which will be used as fuel in winter. The bands of bark are fixed together and left to dry on a bamboo stand.

During paper-making, the bark is pressed in fast-flowing water to make it supple and remove its black skin. The operation takes several hours in summer, and a day in winter. For this purpose, stone dykes have to be built on either side of a quiet stretch of river to obtain the correct conditions. The stems must also be scraped with a knife to complete the cleaning process and to remove not only the black outer bark, but also the underlying green.

The resulting white fibres are dried in the sun for three or four days and then, after being soaked again for about twelve hours, are boiled in an alkaline bath. This operation lasts for about five hours. It is essential because it softens the fibres and removes from them any non-cellulose matter such as tannin. Formerly, a solution of water and ash (from wood, rice straw, reed or buckwheat) was used for this purpose. From the 1920s onwards, chemical products progressively replaced ash despite the harsh treatment they inflict on the fibres. At Ino, near Tosa, the old method is still used in which an ash solution is added one hour before the end of the bath. It is not until the fibres are soft enough to be torn apart by hand that the heating process is finished.

After cooling, alkaline substances are drained off by washing in running water (half a day in summer, two or three nights in winter). This is often completed by bleaching for about four days in the sun or in light reflected from snow.

Immediately after this, the final impurities are removed by hand. This must be done in very cold water to avoid any possible change to the fibres. Balls the size of melons are regularly prepared and drained during this process.

Beating these balls requires the greatest care; the fibres must never be cut, only frayed. Hand beating is still advised (and vital for *gampi*) although machines are increasingly being used. The balls are put on a flat stone or block of wood and beaten using oak sticks or beaters. This work is generally done by women after their day's work. The operation, which lasts about thirty minutes, is always an occasion for cheerful singing, which varies from region to region.

The final operation involves defining the correct consistency of the paper pulp, adding the exact quantity of mucilage and turning it into a sheet of paper.

Fibres ready for pulping

Cleaning the fibres

Beating machine *of the naginata type (the beating scythes beneath the cover resemble the blades of Japanese halberds).*

Bleaching in the river

Traditional beaters

A frame with a sieve attached is plunged into the vat to pick up the pulp. This operation is carried out in two stages. When the pulp is lifted for the first time, the surface area of the sheet of paper is determined. The second time, its thickness is established by making the liquid flow in all four directions to spread out the fibres before the water is forced out. This operation is repeated several times, depending on the thickness required. The sieve is then taken out of the frame and the sheet of paper cut.

The sheets of paper are then stacked and the pile is pressed gradually to expel excess water. Too much pressure or too violent a pressure may damage the paper. Seventy percent of the water is removed during a single night's draining. Finally, the sheets of paper are brushed onto a wooden plank to dry in the sun, or are spread out on a metal drier inside the workshop. The surface exposed to the sun will be the wrong side of the paper, and the surface flattened against the wood or the drier, which will be smoother, is considered to be the right side. The brush used must be long and supple, and generally made of goat's hair, although certain papers require even greater softness. These are then "massaged" with a pad identical to those used by print artists. When drying is finished, the sheets of paper are inspected, sorted and cut before packaging for dispatch.

Paper making

Far left,
top to bottom:
Heating kozo.

Spreading the pulp.

Traditional pressing.

Left,
top to bottom:
*Depositing the sheets
of paper.*

*Forceful extraction of
water in between pulp
spreading.*

Drying in the sun.

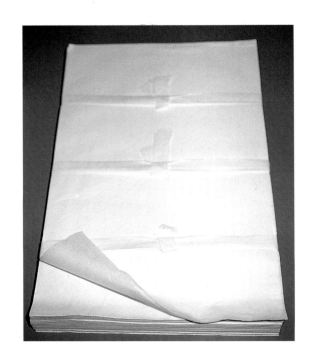

**Packing sheets
of paper**

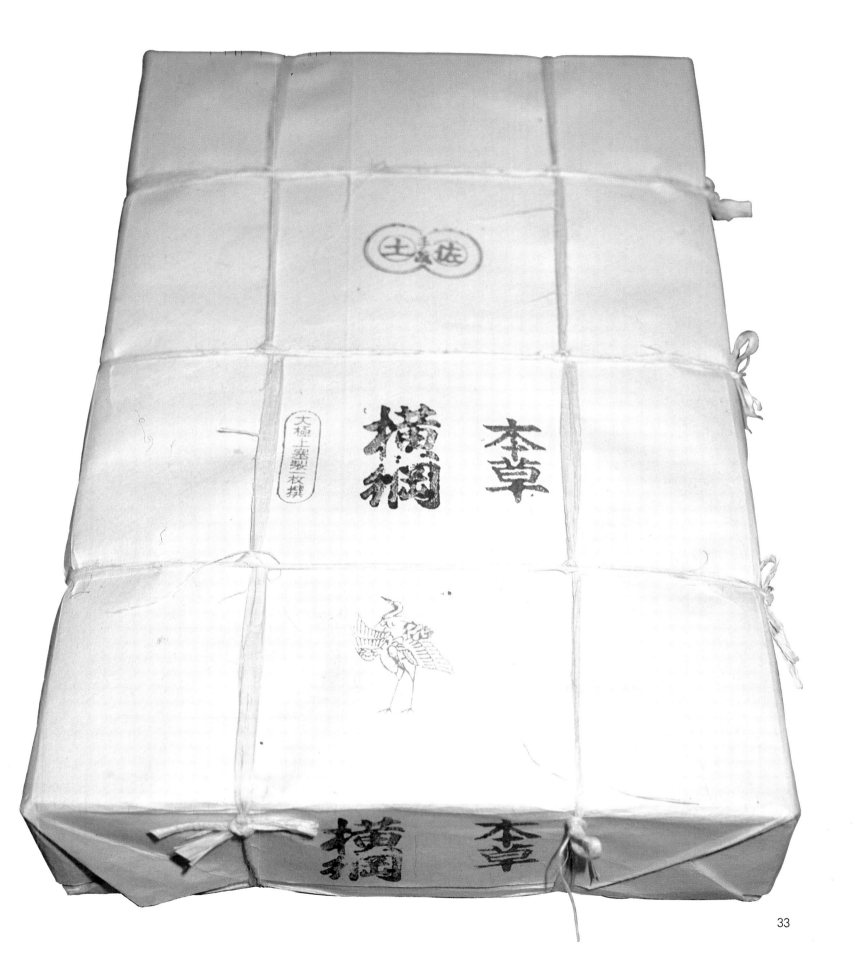

33

Paper of the gods, the gods of paper

From the time when paper was introduced into Japan, the priests of the *shinto* religion were fascinated by its beauty, purity and perfection. Since these qualities were also attributed to the gods, the folding of paper henceforth became symbolic of prayer and offering.

Although the etymology is different, the identical pronunciation of *kami* (paper) and *kami* (*shinto* deity) produced in the ancient Japanese an emotional association between these two words. Since the idea of purity is inextricably linked with that of virginity, they considered natural paper to be both a symbol of bliss on earth and also the very essence of *shinto*. Thus, spotless paper was the ideal medium of expression for divine nature. When folded, it became the sign of its presence. Paper was easy to shape and easy to destroy, which suggested the seasonal cycle of life and death. Once burnt, paper enabled rebirth, as in the case of *shinto* shrines which are rebuilt exactly as before every twenty years. The folding of paper was thus perfectly adapted to annual celebrations and to fertility rites in particular.

Under the sign of the deities

The *shinto* deities, the *kami*, reside in two separate worlds. The first, that of the primordial deities, is celestial and luminous. These superior *kami* engendered the myriads of *kami* in nature, who live in the more humble world of humans. The links between

Opposite:
Buddhist papier-mâché

Papier-mâché tumbling dolls representing Saint Daruma (Bodhidharma) are frequently found in traditional toy workshops. This Buddhist saint, founder of the Chan *(Zen) sect, decided to meditate for nine years at the foot of a tree, to attain enlightenment. So as not to give in to sleep, he cut off his eyelids and threw them away. The first tea plants grew out of this mutilation. Thus each Daruma has white eyes, and the pupils are painted on one by one when a wish is made.*

these two worlds are the high mountains, large trees, and any tree-like vertical structure, such as the main pillar of a house.

To show their sacred nature, these mediators between gods and men were encircled by a taboo rope, the *shimenawa*, made of twisted rice straw supplemented with fibres of hemp and strips of cloth. These ropes were also attached to the branches of certain evergreen trees, or to others which were believed to be the home of a *kami*. The bleached fibres of mulberry bark which were sometimes used for this purpose were also excellent for making paper.

In the 8th and 9th centuries, as techniques of paper-making were developing, strips of folded paper took the place of the cloth strips. The ritual use of paper spread, to the extent that in the 9th century these cut and folded strips could be found on the ceremonial aprons of the *sumo* wrestlers, where they represented the mythical combat of the gods. In those days they were made of strong paper, but later folded silk was used instead at the opening ceremonies of fights.

Cult objects

On view in the shrine itself are two objects made of strips of folded paper fixed to a staff which play an important part in the ceremony. They are the *gohei* and the *harai-gushi*.

The *gohei* is both a symbolic offering and an indication of the presence of the deity in the shrine. There are some twenty ways of folding it, all based on a zigzag, with each having its own esoteric significance. The *kami* are supposed to find the most complex and decorative ones particularly enchanting.

The *harai-gushi* is an instrument of purification and exorcism, which the priest uses to "sweep" the space above the congregation three times. One end of the staff bears a large number of white folded papers along about a metre of its length. Formerly, this staff was simply a mulberry branch, and the paper was made of hemp.

Instead of the *harai-gushi*, a simple branch of *sakaki*, the sacred *shinto* tree, can be decorated with paper and used to conduct a ceremony to communicate with the gods.

Above, opposite and overleaf:
Sacred *shinto* rope

The shimenawa takes its name from shiri-kumi-no-nawa, the sacred shinto rope. It was invented by the god-soothsayer Futotama in mythological times. The Sun Goddess Amaterasu, appalled by the wickedness of her brother, took refuge in a cave, thus depriving the world of her majestic light. Having made her see reason, Futotama forbade entry to the cave forever, barring it with the "taboo rope which prevents any return". The shimenawa is made of rice straw, twisted from right to left. When its form is asymmetric, the thicker part is always on the left.

Above and opposite:
The "heron dance"

Sagi-mai *takes place in Summer, when agricultural work is devoted mainly to rice. The grace of the dance steps is admirably reinforced by the splendour of the costumes. The long neck of the wader which is the dancers' headdress, is made of papier-mâché, while the frame for the wings is hung with white paper.*

Dolls, charms and amulets – divine protection

The *kami* govern the wind, the rain, the crops – all natural phenomena which are feared and respected. They are also concerned with major life events: birth, birthdays, examinations, marriage, illness, etc. Individual *kami* are venerated at each of these important moments of existence: the faithful pray, visit shrines and perform magical practices using paper amongst other materials. The sacred nature of ritual or symbolic folding is augmented by the spirit of purity with which the paper is imbued, and by the absolute necessity of purification. Naturally, a great variety of charms and talismans, made of or wrapped in paper, have been used throughout the ages to the financial profit of the shrines.

Gofu are amulets sold to bring health and good luck. They generally bear the names of the shrine where they are bought and the deity venerated, but many only bear an inscription in red stating their intended purpose. For example, this may be to ensure protection against fire or road accidents, or to bring about the hoped-for conception of a child. To avoid soiling by impure hands, they are attached to a short stick or wrapped in paper, then taken to the small family altar where they will remain. Originally, such amulets were made of hemp and cloth.

From quite early on, the human figure was also used in paper form as a magical aid. *Kata-shiro*, pieces of white paper usually folded in the shape of a doll, are still very popular in certain remote regions of Japan where they are used to ward off evil influences. They are often arranged in houses in groups of eight dolls representing the eight spatial directions to be protected. Others, like *nade-ningyo*, are effigies which are rubbed over the body to treat it or to absorb the demons of illness. A simple cutout in the shape of a *kimono* with the owner's name and date of birth may suffice, but on the island of Shikoku, a real papier mâché statuette is preferred. Twice a year, in Spring and on New Year's Eve, these articles of folded paper are thrown into fast-flowing water, or burned, and other dolls are made for the months to come. An important condition is that the paper must be bought from a shrine or the doll purified by priests before it is used.

Another custom which is even more frequently practised is that of consulting oracles. Each shrine is

Harai-gushi

Scene from kabuki *theatre relating the story of the mythical hero Yamato Takeru. The god, on the right, orders the priest to use his* harai-gushi *to chase away demons.*

Below right:
Ceremonies carried out by the yamabushi monks

This sect of ascetics who live in the mountains is essentially Buddhist, but borrows numerous objects from shinto. *Before any ceremony, the space is purified by the symbols of purity: the salt and paper of the* kami.

Below left:
**Esoteric folded
shape**

*The presence of a god
in the shrine is always
indicated by the* gohei.
*Folded shapes based on
a zigzag are made by
priests versed in the
esotericism of shapes.
They are sometimes
made using coloured
paper, and even sheets
of brass, but white
paper still remains the
ideal material for*
gohei.

Protective charm

These charms for the protection of houses are made of rice stalks for the Gion festival at Kyoto.

Right:
Instrument of purification

The harai-gushi *is the typical* shinto *instrument of purification. The priest uses it to sanctify a space and chase away demons. When not in use, it is placed on a pedestal near the altar.*

Opposite:
Amulet (gofu)

Amulet *(gofu)*

provided with prediction boxes. A bamboo stick is picked at random out of the box and this entitles the enquirer to a small oracle. Once unfolded, the *o-mikuji* predicts very great happiness, a little happiness or misfortune. After reading the oracles, the faithful roll them up and tie them to the branches of the trees at the shrine in the hope of confirming or averting the prediction.

Holy Buddhist writings

Buddhism, an imported religion, became established in Japan in the 6th century. Its attraction was immediate, as it is the expression of civilisation itself. In addition to statues and monumental architecture, it gave Japanese princes their greatest treasure: writing. Japanese paper naturally became the medium for memory, and above all, the vehicle for the sacred word. The magnificence of its rites was echoed by the sumptuousness of paper. Nothing was neglected in reflecting the richness of Buddhist mysteries. Copying sacred texts became an art which went beyond the simple teaching of the monks. It penetrated the world of the aristocracy and took on the affectations of the imperial court. Special ranges of materials, colours and inks were created for the purpose. The paper had to be thick and blue to show off to advantage the ideograms whose written forms were highlighted in gold or silver powder. Later, gold or silver was sprayed in subtle clouds on backgrounds of dark blue or violet paper, or applied as silver or gold leaf. Another category of coloured paper was reserved for Buddhism: pulp for this was taken from the *kihada*, a plant used in dyeing. These sheets of yellow paper only had to be seen for their religious significance to be understood.

When the imperial mill at Kanya ceased production of luxury paper in the 11th century and turned to making recycled paper, the aristocracy seized on this new material to write sutras in memory of departed friends. The ink in the recycled pulp gave a light or dark grey hue to the paper which was greatly appreciated for its "natural" colour. Indian ink used in calligraphy added its sooty hues to give the whole an infinity of solemn, poetic and melancholy nuances. All this corresponded perfectly to the emotional character of the Heian period, but several decades later recycled

Votive dolls

The origin of nagashi-bina *probably goes back to the 15th century. The most common form consists of two dolls dressed in paper kimonos, arranged on a circular bed of rice straw. In this couple, the man is always on the left of his wife. The decoration of their red kimonos, printed with stylised white flowers, is reminiscent of the peach tree blossom, a symbol of marital harmony and feminine delicacy. They are arranged on the family altar at the time of the Festival of Girls on 3rd March, replacing the former dolls whose protection has lapsed. They are then thrown into fast-flowing water, taking bad luck and evil thoughts with them.*

Paper in popular religion

Top left:
O-mikuji oracles.

Top right:
Ornament decorating the ceremonial "costume" of Tosa fighting dogs.

Bottom left:
Tanabata *festival. The "festival of stars", celebrated on 7th July, is based on a legend concerning the love between the stars Vega and Altaïr. To wish them happiness, the Japanese hang narrow strips of coloured paper on bamboo branches in their garden. Young people write romantic poems on them.*

Bottom right:
Yamabushi *ceremony. Offerings and* gohei.

Sake offerings

The gods love alcohol. The custom of offering them barrels of sake lives on, especially at the shrines close to trading districts.

Kirigami

Paper cutouts are also part of the expression of shinto. They are most often associated with the family altar (kami-dana) where symbols of good augury appear. Here they decorate the stage used for sacred dances in one of the oldest shrines in Japan, Takachiho-jinja, on the island of Kyushu. Ninigi took possession of the land in the name of the Sun Goddess. A sacred rope can be seen under this border, decorated with strips of green and white and red and white.

paper fell into common use and lost its specific Buddhist associations.

Gods of paper

Buddhism only produced a few outstanding folded paper shapes. However, the religious syncretism which was the rule for many centuries allowed them to coexist with the ritual objects of the *shinto* religion. *Kami* paper could be found side by side with Buddhist statues, and it is likely that the few esoteric folded paper shapes of Buddhism were only a late development of *shinto* models. Conversely, the plastic art invented and developed by Buddhist monks gave rise to a mini *shinto* statuary, usually made from papier-mâché in the image of popular deities, like the fox, the emblem of tradesmen. From the 16th century onwards, the two religions were enriched with figures from Taoism and Chinese Confucianism. The seven gods of happiness often competed with the ancestral gods and Buddhist saints for pride of place on the family altar and in displays on booths. They were made of papier-mâché like the small Buddhist "tumbling" dolls depicting Saint Daruma. Each region also produced its secondary figures, who ensured a healthy and prosperous life. Local legends or edifying stories based on real situations were always a source of inspiration for original creations. It was thus that a little servant girl, Hoko-san, became famous on the island of Shikoku. Her mistress, a beautiful princess, had fallen gravely ill. The young servant nursed her mistress back to health with such devotion that she contracted the illness herself. She then had to withdraw from the world to avoid re-infecting the royal household, leaving to posterity an image of sacrifice and complete devotion. From then on, her figurine accompanied all wishes for recovery and hopes of cure, not only on that island, but also in many other regions of Japan.

Folded Buddhist shape

A folded shape belonging to the esoteric Tendai sect representing the element of Water.

Opposite:
A Buddhist reading

Paper as ceremonial art

In former times, it was unthinkable to prepare for a ceremony without seeking the favour of the gods. Many enduring customs draw their originality from these early rituals. Some have a direct connection with religion, such as those relating to marriages or funerals, and other more profane customs developed from them, such as the art of the gift, or good luck symbols. All have in common the profound idea that everyday life should be rendered sacred. Paper, a symbol of purity when natural or white in colour, became a ceremonial object when it was coloured. Court protocol linked it to its own rites, benevolence requiring that correspondence be looked after like an offering. Poetry could no longer do without colour to underline its emotions.

The colours of paper

Originally, the paper which came from China was too imperfect a material to withstand the voraciousness of insects. As a result, it was often necessary to dye paper in order to preserve it. The Koreans are said to have been the first to experiment with this technique, closely followed by the Persians. If the accounts of the imperial Sassanid court of the 6th century can be believed, a fastidious monarch, who could not stand the odour of parchment, only used paper dyed with saffron and perfumed with rose water. In imitation of continental customs, and to improve the keeping qualities of their first types of paper, the Japanese adopted the practice of blending with the pulp

Opposite:
Wrapping paper

Printing by superimposing dyes. The variable adhesiveness of the final layer of dye on the gilded coat creates this spectacular cloud effect. The colours are obtained using successive baths.

Right and opposite:
Dyed paper

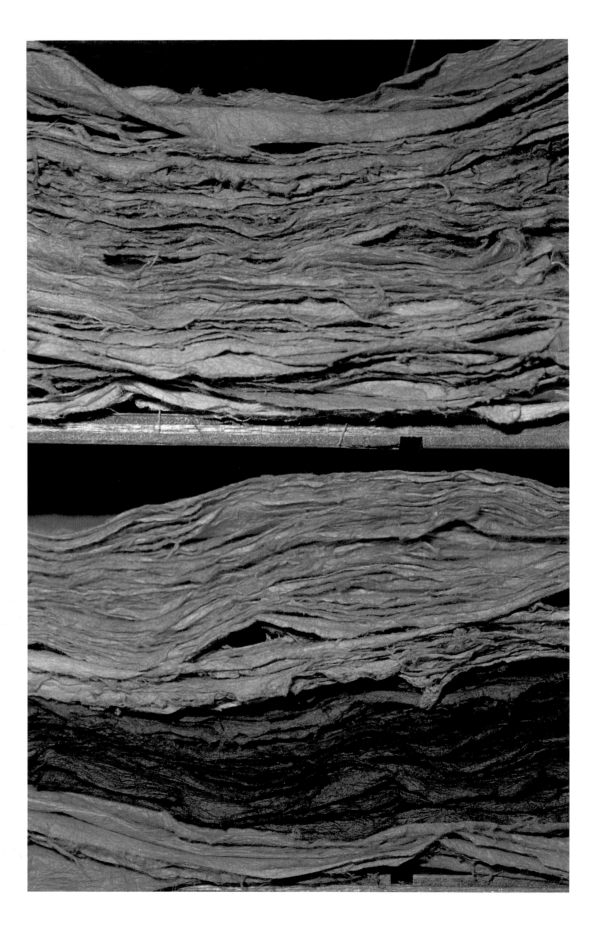

decoctions of plants used in dyeing which were known to repel insects. These dyes were also a guarantee against mould during the monsoons. They protected not only the paper but also certain types of wood so, for example, the red paint made from cinnabar, which was originally used to decorate *shinto* buildings, also had protective qualities.

The treasure from the Horyuji temple at Nara contains hemp papers dyed in the frame and by printing. Although dating from the 8th century, they are very well preserved and still serve as a reference for dyeing today. The palette is extraordinarily varied, as much in colour (yellow, red, pink, blue, brown, green) as in techniques of dyeing (direct colouring of fibres, printing by stencil, inclusion of different materials...). From the introduction of Chinese culture, colour was linked to protocol. The rank of state servants was identified by the colour of their headdress and the ribbons on their clothing. *Shinto* shrines followed suit, reserving specific colours for themselves.

The plants in most frequent use at that time were the *kihada*, whose yellow colour, *ai*, dyed both paper and cloth, was appreciated by Buddhist monks, the *murasaki*, which yielded the Japanese colour *par excellence* in its thousand hues of violet, as well as dogrose, jasmine and sappanwood. Minerals – in particular iron oxide – were used for dyeing at an early stage.

This palette was enriched with a vast number of hues with the advent of the Heian court. Avid for splendour and novelty, princes clamoured endlessly for new emotions. Roots, leaves, berries, fruits and walnuts were used for dyeing both paper and cloth. The brilliance of the "Chinese" colours of the Nara period was replaced by the subtlety of the nuances of colour prized by Heian princes – the very essence of Japanese aesthetics. The intangible subtlety of hue of the countryside around the capital, always filtered by morning mists, became the ultimate chromatic reference. This fascination with subdued shades found concrete form in the art of *kasane-no-irome*, the overlapping of colours. This art was originally applied to clothing. Women at court wore several *kimonos*, one on top of the other, each sleeve showing slightly beyond the others to create a harmony of colours which was adapted to the seasons. The imperial princesses wore up to twelve at a time and their

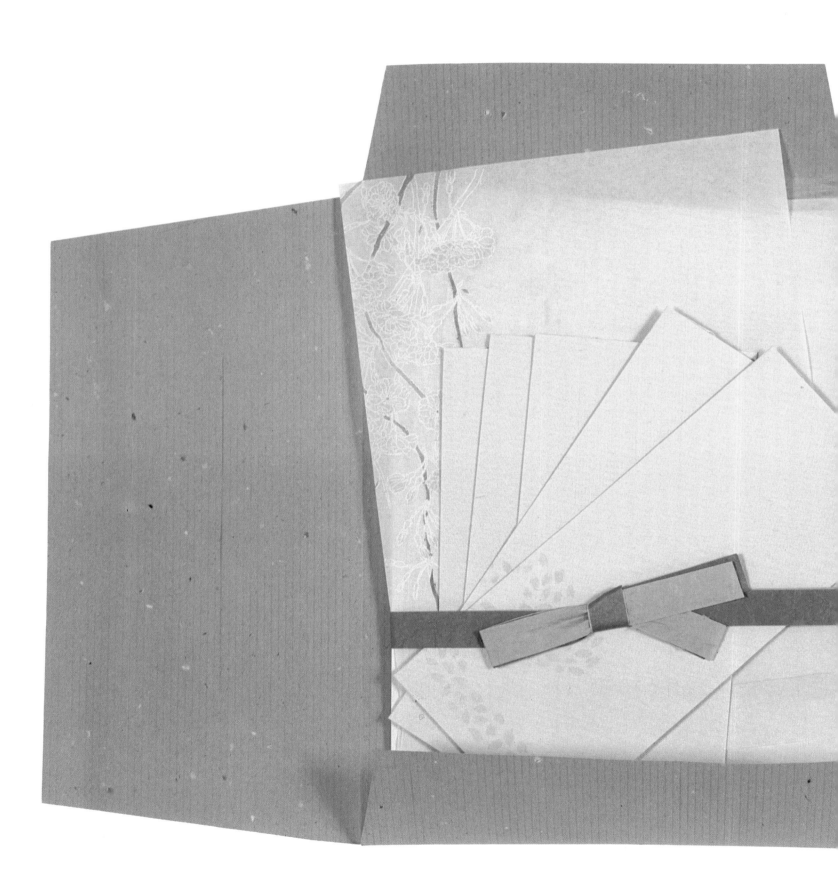

Wrapping paper for chopsticks

Left:
Writing paper

昨日もひらひら
今朝もひらひら
今もひらひら
桜ひらひら
千散り万散り
千万散り散り
散っても散っても
散り尽きない

display of colours soon inspired other craftsmen, many of them paper-makers. These highborn ladies were also fascinated by very thin coloured paper, which was almost transparent. It was in this spirit that the art of collage soon became indispensable to poetry. Cards used for poems were a delicate assembly of paper of varied hues, playing on the effects of gradations, clouds or abrupt cutout shapes. The famous *Collection of Thirty-six Poets*, dating from the 16th century, is a good example. During the same period, Saburozaemon Aki created *Tosa-nana-iro-gami*, a collection of seven coloured sheets of paper for making poem cards.

Three main methods of dyeing are still used by craftsmen.

In *suki-zome*, the fibres are dyed before the pulp is made. They are beaten and drained before being plunged into a dye bath for a day, and then into a mordant bath for another half-day. The pulp is then prepared, and the paper made according to classical rules.

In *tsuke-zome*, finished sheets of paper are plunged into a dye bath, then a mordant bath, before being dried. Generally, the operation is repeated at least three times to obtain better colour quality. This is preferable to a single bath of saturated colour.

In *hiki-zome*, dyeing is carried out using a brush on one or both surfaces of the paper. A variant called *fuki-zome* consists of spraying the colour onto the sheet of paper.

Other processes are used to create decorative paper. Marbled paper, similar to Western handmade paper, is called "ink floating". It dates from the 12th century and was used primarily for poem cards, care being taken never to cover the entire surface in order to leave enough space for writing. Later, in the Edo period, the whole surface and sometimes the reverse side of the sheet was covered in marbled patterns. The craftsmen used a brush for colouring, alternately applying colours and oil to the pulp. Dispersal was achieved by blowing.

Two other quite similar techniques arose from textile craftsmanship. "Tie dyeing" and "fold dyeing" were mainly used in the manufacture of bags, cushions, book jackets or other useful objects. The first method requires very solid creased paper which can withstand being tied before dyeing. The second needs very thin paper to preserve the marks of its folds clearly, so that they are saturated with colour when unfolded. Originally, when this technique was used for dyeing cloth in the

Dyeing sheets of paper using a brush

Paper used for folded shapes often needs to be different colours on the front and back, in order to emphasise the opposition of decorative folds or to enhance more naturalistic forms.

Opposite:
Tsutsumi using a flat knot

This system should be used on all unrepeatable occasions such as weddings or funerals.

Noshi-zutsumi

Folded noshi *shape (top right) and* tsutsumi *knot. The white or light-coloured strings are always on the left of the loop.*

8th century, craftsmen used planks of wood which were engraved with symmetrical patterns and drilled with holes to allow the colour to pass through. The paper-making centre at Kurodani, near Kyoto, specialised in these treatments of bright and popular papers.

The art of dyeing includes two spectacular techniques. The older dates from the end of the Nara period and consists of inserting fibres, usually dyed with indigo, between two sheets of paper. This operation is carried out directly in the pulp vat. As soon as a sheet of paper is raised up on the sieve, the coloured fibres are arranged on its surface and a second white sheet is laid over it. The resulting effect is rather like light clouds. In the 14th century, the emperor Go Daigo had paper made with ivy added to the pulp. From this time on, it became the custom to include seasonal plants in the paper. In the Edo period, the process spread and developed. The skeletons of certain leaves, bark strips and pine needles were used, as were gold or silver leaf or mica powder. Very recently, the Gifu centre began to include insects and butterflies in its promotional literature.

Paper symbols

In spite of the magnificence of coloured paper, white paper remained the rule for solemn occasions. White paper folded in the shape of butterflies was associated with marriage rites and symbolised the communication of future husbands with the guardian deities of their families, clans or neighbourhood shrine, as well as the purity appropriate to this important stage of life. The whiteness of the male and female butterfly represented the inherent virginity of this new life, just like the bride's *kimono*. They are attached by gold and silver ribbons to the bottles of sake served at ritual libations during which the union is consecrated. From the end of the ceremony onwards, the newlyweds become "human" again and the young woman dons a sumptuous coloured *kimono*. These charming articles of folded paper are in fact a development of the paper corks decorating the *sake* bottles which are arranged around the family altar.

Folded paper articles were, and still are, made by masters whose knowledge was passed on orally, and because of this they were only made on very formal

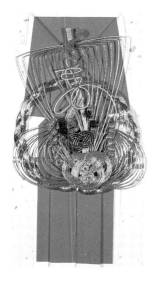

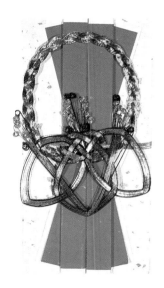

Wedding *tsutsumi*

It is customary to present the bride with the nine objects that symbolise her status as a wife and accomplished housewife, along with the symbols of happiness: seaweed, bonito, abalone, cuttlefish, silver, linen thread, fan and coins for sake. Each object is thus presented in a votive folded shape decorated with very complex tsutsumi.

**Ritual wedding
object**

Kegs of sake *decorated
with votive butterflies.
The male butterfly, on
the left, is ornamented
with a crane.*

Keg of *sake*

The female butterfly is decorated with a tortoise. These two mizuhiki *animals are symbols of longevity.*

Wedding wig

*Paper ribbons are used
in the wedding wig.*

Mizuhiki

*A mizuhiki lobster for
a New Year
decoration. For all
those bowed with age,
it is a wish for
longevity.*

ceremonial occasions. Most of the techniques were passed on by two priestly families, the Yoshida and the Matsu-ura, who belonged to the *shinto* sect of the Great Shrine of Ise. In the past, paper was so rare and expensive that it was barely compatible with a pastime. It even appeared to be radically unsuited to the "vulgarity" of ordinary acts. Folding paper was thus a formal act requiring strict etiquette, and codes of use developed. This was the case in the Muromachi period (1333-1573) with, for example, *origami-tsuki*, which was placed on a work of art after its appraisal. This folded paper was none other than a certificate folded in two, but it expressed the fact that the object had become sacred. It should be noted that when doing his job, the expert held a piece of paper folded in half in his mouth to prevent his breath from defiling the sheet of paper or the lacquer.

Under certain circumstances, folded paper could be a substitute for rare objects. This was the case with the folded form called *noshi*. At the end of the 12th century, it replaced the parting gift which was always to offered to a warrior leaving on a campaign. This present originally consisted of a thin slice of *noshi-awabi*, a shellfish also called the "ear of the sea" which, once dried, did not decompose. This token of long life and protection against evil was carefully wrapped in a sheet of paper. In time the shellfish became rare, and was replaced by other items. Then it was replaced by a strip of paper dyed yellow which was placed in a flattened cone of white, or red and white, paper and fastened by decorative twisted paper strings. These *mizuhiki* ribbons were crimson and white for important ceremonies, red and white (or red and gold) for exceptional circumstances, and gold and silver for marriage and joyful ceremonies. By contrast, for funerals they were black and white, blue and white or simply white. In this case, *noshi* were never used – ribbons alone decorated the gift. The same applied to offerings of fish, seafood and eggs. The last category of *mizuhiki* was multicoloured and was only used for informal decorations. These practices all live on but, since the 1930s, printed *noshi* have all too often replaced folded paper sculptures.

Initially, *noshi* was always white, as the rules of propriety required virgin paper for any offering, even when profane. The very idea of the gift involved an intermediary between giver and receiver. It would have

been inappropriate to offer something directly by hand, and the wrapping of a gift showed that it was a gift from the heart. The rules of etiquette, drawn up at a later date, specify that the nature of the gift should be written on the upper part of an attached sheet, with the giver's name written below. For very important occasions, the wrapping invariably had to consist of two sheets laid back to back, with the softer or shinier surface indicating the right side of the paper. The *noshi* is generally placed on the top right-hand side of the parcel, but is sometimes slipped inside it, as is the case when the gift is a basket of fruit.

The paper ribbons which are used to accompany gifts were introduced at the start of the 7th century when a Japanese diplomat brought some back from China. Their main function was to prevent impurities from entering the parcel. Originally, they were simply twisted, but the Japanese quickly invented the art of starching them so that they could be made thinner and more rigid. This also introduced a further symbolic meaning – once tied, the ribbons could not be untied without losing their rigidity, making them especially

Ceremonial costume

Lady from the Heian court wearing a ceremonial costume consisting of superimposed kimonos. The overlapping strips of the sleeves and collars influenced the art of paper dyeing and the creation of colour charts used in the making of poem cards.

Modern wrapping based on the use of coloured paper

relevant on sad or significant occasions which should never be repeated, such as funerals or weddings. Numerous ways of tying the strings were also invented to emphasise the positive nature of the gifts. One of these consisted in rolling the ends of the ribbons upon themselves, to represent the foam of the waves continuously washed up on the beach. Other symbolic shapes taken from the world of the warrior, such as the bow, are a good omen and are used on more ceremonial occasions than the simple knot reserved for ordinary *noshi*.

These different varieties of folds and ropes were given a hierarchical order according to strict formal rules drawn up by numerous schools of etiquette. One of the oldest, the Ogasawara school, remains associated with many folded forms which bear its name. They all have multiple folds whose purpose was to intensify the rigidity and magnificence of the objects. This can be seen in the work entitled *Models of all the styles of folded forms of the Ogasawara school*, published in 1910. Sixty-five kinds of basic fold, from butterflies for weddings to wrappings on a gold background, were taught at this school, which was responsible for etiquette at the *shogun*'s court from the 13th century onwards. It was also renowned for the quality of its methods in areas as important as the handling of the sabre or the firing of a bow. It was consulted in particular in the Edo period, when it published a manual intended exclusively for women.

Another famous school of the Muromachi period, responsible for etiquette at the *shogun*'s court, was that of the Ise family. This family published a work in 1764 called the *Hoki*, which described seventeen types of ceremonial wrapping, in particular for marriages and *gempuku*, the celebration of coming of age. Sadatake Ise had *Notes on wrapping and ceremonial knots* printed in 1865.

All these folded forms go back to the Heian period, the period when everything borrowed from Chinese culture was made truly Japanese. Official letters containing details of appointments or military orders – originally simple missives folded lengthways – had subtleties in their folds to represent the ranks or circumstances involved. This practice of folding then passed on to the private sphere of homes or women's quarters, where the folding of love poems required the greatest care. At the start of the period, the term *ori-*

kami (folded paper) was used to designate such artefacts, but then, considering their complexity, the term *ori-kata* (way of folding) was preferred, until the word *ori-gata* (folded form) became widespread, thus indicating that the folding of paper had generated more figurative forms. Many of these folded forms had notches or cuts in them as decoration, and the term for this technique was *kiri-kami* (cutout paper), but it was not until 1880 that the word ori-gami appeared to describe the playful folded forms which will be examined in the chapter entitled "Paper games". Nowadays, these ceremonial folded forms from *noshi* to prestige wrapping are referred to as *tsutsumi* or *ori-gata*. As a mark of courtesy and good manners, wrapping is an indispensable part of Japanese life today. Japan consumes such a quantity of paper that the authorities considered limiting its use in order to reduce significantly the importation of paper pulp from the West. The measure did not work. The Japanese custom of giving presents twice a year, at the start of July (in the hope that older people will withstand the hot summer months well) and at the end of the year, is too firmly entrenched in the Japanese mentality and economy to be changed or abolished. The choice of paper and the designs printed on it are also a way of continually referring to the rhythm of the seasons, without which Japanese society would lose part of its soul. Traditionally white, today's wrapping paper is governed by colour and by the materials of the new paper as soon as it escapes convention to become merely pleasing to the eye. The habit of using layers of coloured paper is developing as rapidly as the new range of objects which can be wrapped in them.

Wrapped fruits

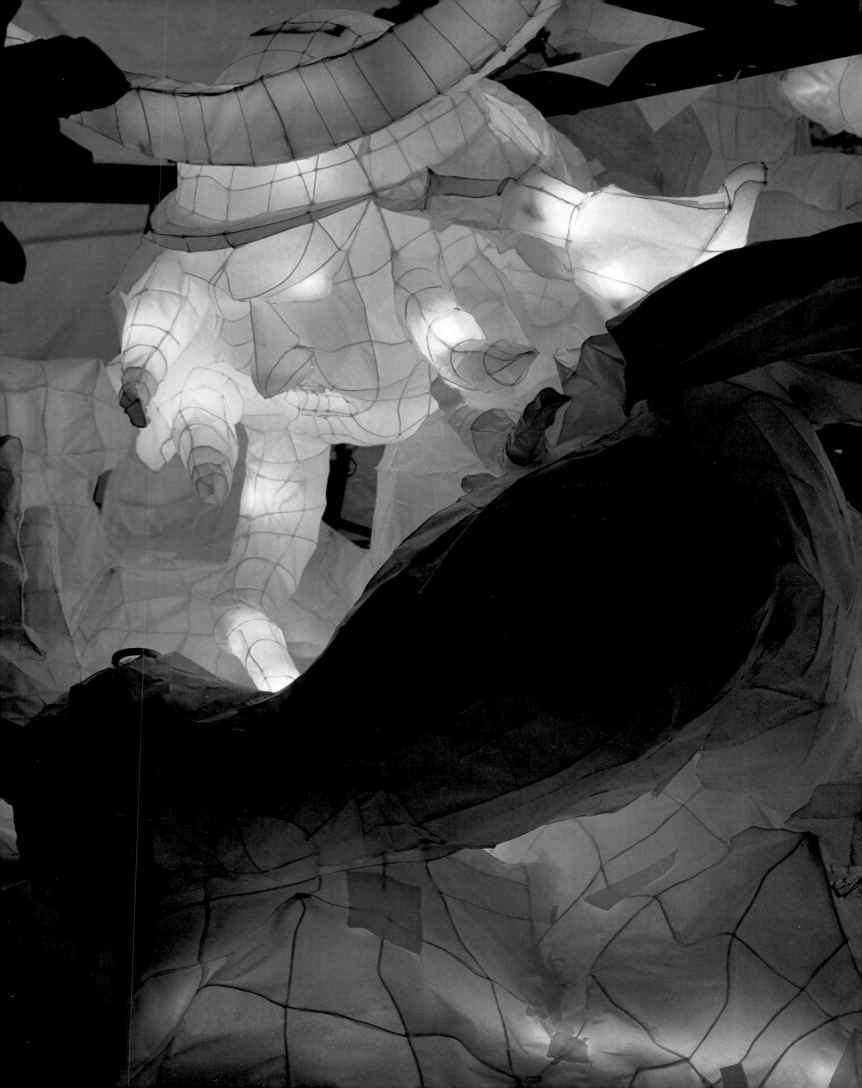

The craftsman's art

Paper in all its forms

From their earliest beginnings, men have always confronted matter. They have loved its nobility and its harsh requirements. From the start, they sought to understand its mystery, often attributing its existence to divine intervention. The Japanese were no exception. Indeed, it could be claimed that they have accentuated its effects more than most. An earthly translator of divine life, the craftsman soon learnt how to rival his masters, without forgetting that he must make them an offering of his work. The only gift he could decently offer the gods was, naturally, his desire for quality. Respect for matter and mastery of the art are the first tools of this requirement. By chance, Japan benefits from two religions which place great importance upon nature and confer a sacred character upon its products. *Shinto* lends its purifying conscience, while Buddhism offers its spiritual loftiness and aesthetic sense, which brings the craftsman close to the artist.

Japanese craftsmanship is extremely varied and works with the special elements of a specific climate and natural world. Many plants only grow in Japan, blessing the country with an exclusive raw material which craftsmen have cultivated assiduously, and paper gains its originality from this. Japan was also fortunate to follow in the historical footsteps of China, an extraordinarily rich and cultivated country with a thousand years' experience. Japan's genius lay in improving this knowledge by transforming it into a typically Japanese creation. Moreover, Japanese craftsmanship has been

Opposite:
Nebuta

A structure made from nebuta *paper. A legend explains its creation. An 8th century lord used paper models in the shape of men, animals and birds to deceive the enemy as to the true size of his army. The subterfuge worked and victory was assured. This is commemorated by a lantern parade bearing the effigy of the "heroes" in paper. Later, these lanterns, called nebuta, became illuminated sculptures measuring ten metres in height, which were carried through the streets by dozens of men in festival costume. This summer festival takes place before harvest begins. From a religious point of view, its primary purpose is to rouse the people's spirit from the languor of summer so that everyone is ready for the hard work awaiting them.*

71

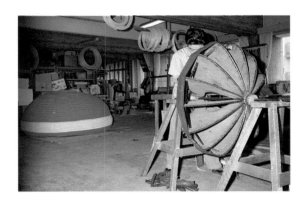

Above:
**Making Gifu
lanterns**

*Ribs arranged on a
frame take the very
thin paper which is the
hallmark of these
summer lanterns.*

endowed with the refinement and excitement of its own troubled history. Jewels are often extracted from mud, and the archipelago has had its share of grief. Japanese culture thus fostered the use of the most perfect objects, which in time became indispensable to its daily life.

If the Nara and Heian periods were marked by the discovery of art and its methods, and the Muromachi and Momoyama periods left the names of inspired artists and craftsmen to posterity, the Edo period learned to promote the wide range of their creations. Perhaps more than any other, this 260 year period of peace revealed the true Japanese genius, far from the luxury of the temples, castles and the court. The people themselves were the initiators and tireless users of crafted objects. Since external influences were proscribed, Japanese culture could only be self-fertilising, perfecting or redeveloping even the least of its achievements. Contemporary Japan's highly inventive sense of "design" has its roots in this creative profusion, where the absolute search for quality was the craftsman's first impulse.

Modern problems, such as ergonomics, storage and miniaturisation were resolved during the Edo period. The craftsman of the time knew how to work with the qualities of flexibility, and how to fold, stack, roll up and fit paper together in many ways. He added a taste for harmony and a love of the symbol to this pragmatism.

During the Edo period, the development of paper was as dynamic as the common townspeople. Peace gave rise to the new art of the long-distance walk. Sumptuary laws prevented travellers from making journeys by palanquin or on horseback, so they discovered the riches of the countryside on foot. As these trips necessarily lasted a long time, it was important to plan in detail the number of essential objects to take. These necessities had to be very light and not at all cumbersome. A number of accessories were thus recreated using paper. In 1811, the *Practical guide to travelling*, published in Edo, provided a list: a paintbrush case, needles and cotton, a pocket mirror, a fan, a notebook, a comb, hair oil, a lantern, a candle, a lighter, a smoking set, a ball of hemp, a medicine box, inkstone, a purse, a toilet case, a snuffbox, a box for papers and a passport wallet. To this should be added rainwear and a travelling hat.

In these circumstances, oiled or waterproofed paper

Gifu lantern

Lighting a Gifu lantern during the Tenjin festival at Osaka.

came into its own. It shared this fame with the great partner of *washi*: bamboo. The two most typical objects of Japanese craftsmanship, the parasol and the lantern, grew out of the perfect complementary relationship between these materials. The parasol and the lantern had the common link of being designed in harmony with the most outstanding characteristic of *washi*, its pliability. Without the astounding strength of *kozo* fibres, the parasol and the pocket lantern, like the folding fan, would not have become the very symbols of Japan.

The chochin lantern

The Japanese lantern was invented at the beginning of the 14th century, at a time when the use of pine-resin candles was becoming widespread. The lantern

Top left:
Putting up a restaurant lantern

Overleaf:
Lantern craftsman

The lantern craftsman must be an excellent painter and a calligraphist with a steady hand.

Mitama-matsuri

The Festival of Lanterns at Shizuoka. The holy ground of the shrine is completely covered with lanterns, offered in thanksgiving by the faithful to honour the memory of all Japanese dead.

Opposite:
Toro

The Buddhist Sensoji temple in Tokyo is famous for the enormous lanterns adorning its gates. The lantern at the Kaminari gate measures 3.3 m in height and weighs over 100 kg.

also replaced torches and lamps which used fish oil or vegetable wax. From then on, the flame was protected by a quadrangular wooden frame, hung with paper on its four surfaces. Such lanterns were called *andon*. From the 16th century onwards they were fitted with feet, and with a means of transporting them or hanging them permanently on the internal and external walls of houses.

The term "lantern" covers three other basic types of object. The first category includes all kinds of enclosed lamps used in religion. These are referred to as toro irrespective of whether they are stone or bronze lanterns adorning the outside of temples or shrines, paper lanterns bearing temple inscriptions, lanterns for the Festival of the Dead, or the lanterns which are floated on the water at purification ceremonies. Originally they provided light for the monks during their long night-time meditations, or illuminated the altar, as in China.

The second category comprises most of the interior lighting lamps, known as *bombori*. These smaller *andon* are generally round and are placed in the reception room. Originally a simple paper cone concealing the candle, the *bombori* is often many-sided, with a frame covered in paper or thin cloth. To this category of furnishings can be added portable lanterns, which are still used today inside the house. These can be fixed to the wall as detachable lamps and brought to the table at meal times.

The folding lantern (*chochin*) was primarily used in the Edo period. Used by the lowliest and the richest citizen alike, it was vital to city life. It became so important that it figured in a number of popular expressions to describe certain character traits. Thus the unnecessarily idle person was a "lantern alight all day" and any individual who could do nothing for himself was a "lantern-carrier".

Chochin are all folding. For this reason they are often made by craftsmen who specialise in making parasols. The materials are the same: paper, bamboo and glue. For lighting purposes, the paper must be very strong but translucent. It must also be in harmony with the Japanese taste for the tranquillity and serenity of a diffused light after dusk. This is why the choice of paper is of vital importance.

Kozo paper fulfils this requirement. In the Edo period, it was produced mainly in the Gifu regions to supply Kyoto and Osaka, in Odawara to supply the workshops of Edo, in Fukuoka to light the inhabitants of the island of Kyushu, and in Aomori to make the enormous lanterns used for the Nebuta festival. *Mitsumata* paper was also used for lantern paper, but to a considerably lesser degree.

Designed for outside use, the folding lantern became a social object in strictly regimented Edo society. Legislation imposed precise codes of use. State servants or members of large religious institutions, firemen, policemen, monks, the *samurai*, tradesman and even merrymakers frequenting pleasure houses carried lanterns adapted to their station. The names given to them were as numerous as their individual appearances. Trademarks, family coats of arms, and even the shape of the *chochin* were crucial to the identification of night-time strollers, and the police made great use of this information. The same applied to debtors whose payments were due before 31st December, and who

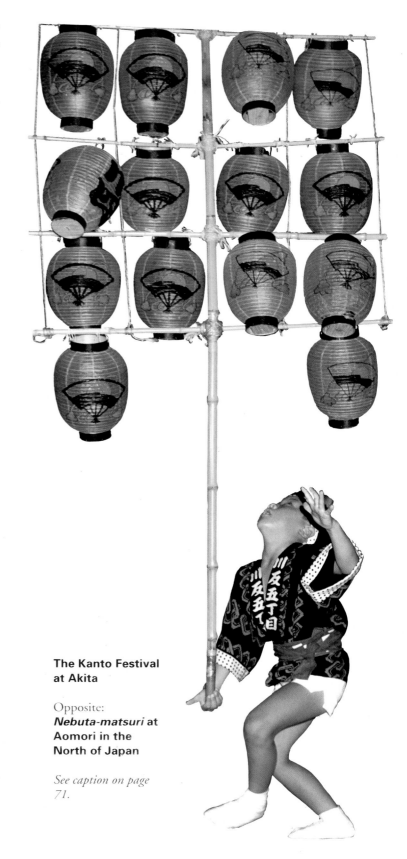

The Kanto Festival at Akita

Opposite:
***Nebuta-matsuri* at Aomori in the North of Japan**

See caption on page 71.

79

Saga lantern

Opposite:
Toro

*Altar lantern in a
Buddhist temple.*

were on the look-out for the dreaded lanterns of the money-lenders. The mere sight of them inspired flight, but there was no need to fear the "lantern-boxes" carried by the admirers of pretty women on their way to the houses of pleasure. In its role as a means of identification, the lantern was sometimes an accessory in war strategy. During an attempted *coup d'état*, the conspirators had a large number of lanterns made bearing the arms of Ikeda Mitsumasa, a particularly well-loved overlord. His coat of arms in the form of a butterfly with outspread wings was visible throughout the streets, giving the impression of popular support, without the overlord being directly involved in the demonstration.

Methods of transporting the *chochin* were as varied as the marks painted on their paper. This can be seen from old domestic lantern boxes. These were made of thick paper or lacquer and hung on the lintels of doors. They were adorned with the family coat of arms in black and with the function of their contents in red. In them, for example, could be found the marriage lantern embossed with the family crest. Since the bride and groom travelled to the place of ceremony on horseback, it was important that the hanging lantern should not be shaken too much by the movement of their mount, and to this effect it was fitted with a flexible telescopic rod to absorb vibrations. A lantern was placed beside its box for use in emergencies such as fires, earthquakes or other catastrophes to light the way as the inhabitants fled. The outer rod which kept it open was shaped something like a bow. This type of lantern was particularly useful to the *samurai* who could place it open on the ground when they needed to draw their swords. The adjacent chest contained the "round lantern for lighting one's way". It was used on the path to the house or in the garden. Like the marriage lantern, it hung from a rod, but this one was shorter and non-telescopic.

In addition to these family lanterns, there were specific *chochin*, such as the knight's lantern which had a long shaft for lighting the way when on horseback, or the "pocket" lantern, which was slipped inside the sleeve or front of the *kimono*. Among the latter, the most famous are the *odawara-jochin*, originally made in the village of Odawara, in a region where the bushes and plants used in paper-making flourished. They are a refined version of the "lantern-boxes" which men

Lantern box

The box bears the household coat of arms.

Opposite:
Cemetery lantern

A Buddhist cemetery at the time of Bon, the Festival of the Dead. This event takes place from the 13th to the 16th of July to welcome the souls of the dead which have returned home. A lantern is placed on the newly-cleaned tomb, which is lit on the eve of the 13th to guide the spirits. This lantern is then taken back to the house and put on the family altar, as it is thought that the souls of ancestors take up residence in the flame of the candle. On the 16th, the old candle is replaced by a new one which lights the visitors' way back to their tombs.

carried when going to Yoshiwara, the courtesan's district. Once drawn together, the upper and lower parts, which were made of wood and metal, formed a closed box around the paper accordion. This system was perfected in the *odawara-jochin* which was made much smaller and was designed to be placed in the sleeve. It became the typical lantern of Edo and, when the fashion for going on long walks began, it could be found everywhere on the Tokaido road, which linked Edo to Kyoto.

Apart from the models linked to purpose or symbolism, the Japanese lamp came in all shapes and sizes for solely decorative purposes. The range is extremely extensive, but the most common are the "round lanterns", oblong lanterns shaped like old coins, cylindrical *odawara-jochin* and their bigger cousins of the same type, the "lantern-gourds" in the shape of a bitter apple, and especially the *gifu-jochin*, whose mere name evokes an image of the lantern. This creation from the region of Gifu uses very thin, transparent paper which is often decorated with floral motifs as a reminder of its original Buddhist use.

The Gifu lantern is typical of another aspect of the Japanese soul, namely its total integration with natural rhythms, and the seasons in particular. In the Japan of former times there was no air-conditioning to counteract the trying heat of summer, and so all the accessories of daily life tended to give the ear and eye an impression of liveliness, transparency and coolness. Small bells tinkled lightly, shutters broke up excessively strong light, the material from which crockery was made evoked the cool water of fast-flowing streams, and vertical paintings brightened shadowy areas with their light, sparkling brushstrokes. The *gifu-jochin* provided the finishing touch to this display of lightness, with its extremely thin, transparent paper.

More recently, craftsmen have tried to develop the lantern in more creative ways, while still preserving its traditional spirit and reusing old techniques. New shapes have been created, such as that designed by Yoshitaka Sasai in Kyoto. For the framework of his lanterns he sometimes uses old lobster pots such as those which were formerly filled with stones to make foundations or dykes. This framework accentuates all the characteristics of the classical lantern. The bamboo strips are much wider to contrast with the transparency of the paper, which is thicker than normal. The

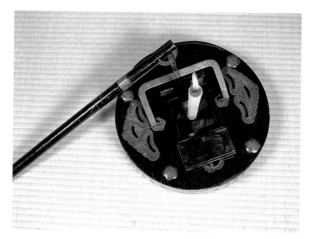

Box lantern and lighting system

Opposite:
Odawara-jochin, the sleeve lantern

According to legend, the fox god's cunning was no longer feared on the roads thanks to this lantern.

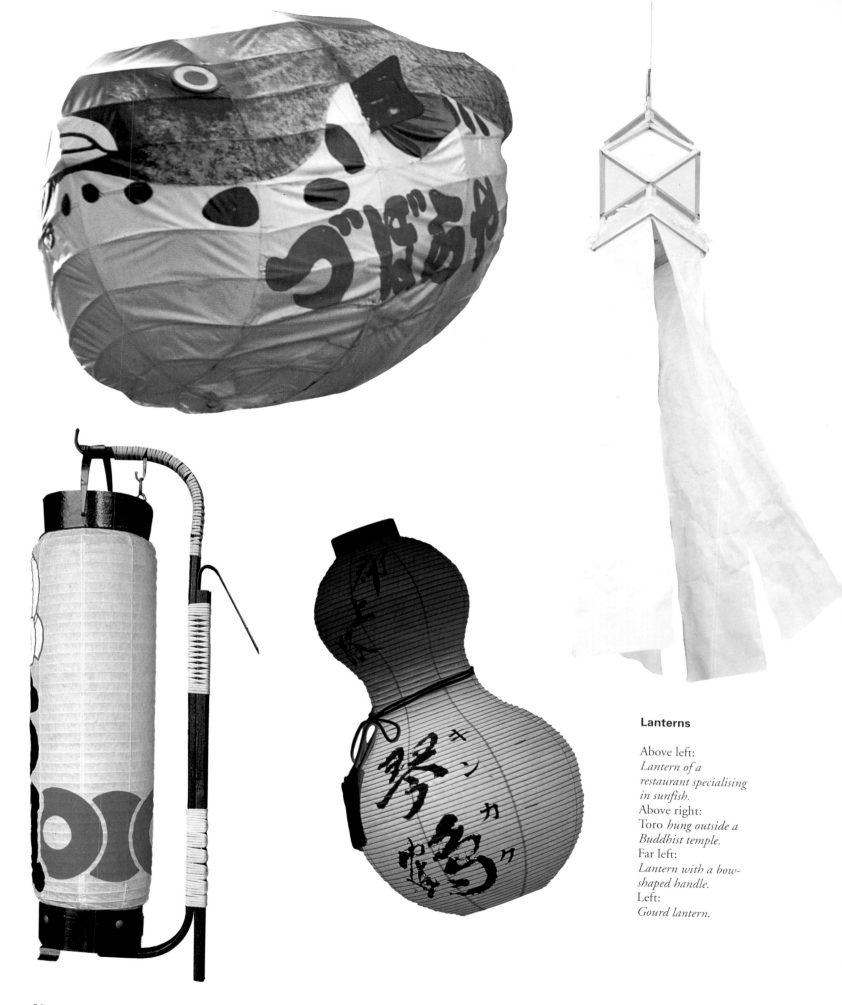

Lanterns

Above left:
Lantern of a restaurant specialising in sunfish.
Above right:
Toro *hung outside a Buddhist temple.*
Far left:
Lantern with a bow-shaped handle.
Left:
Gourd lantern.

Lanterns

Far left:
Bombori from the Edo *period.*
Left:
A lampu, *or Western style standard lamp, made from Gifu paper.*
Below left:
Wall lamp with coat of arms.
Below right:
Child's chochin for the Jizo-Bon *festival.*

Overleaf:
Round restaurant lanterns.

Opposite:
Modern lantern

Lantern by Yoshitaka Sasai from Kyoto. The decoration in persimmon juice darkens with time.

Modern lanterns

The new craftsmen, like Isamu Nogushi, seek to adapt their works to modern architectural space. The designs of the frame are often quite different from those of former times, but washi *remains the best material for transmitting light.*

decoration is remarkable for its simplicity. It consists simply of traces of persimmon juice, applied with a brush. This coating waterproofed the paper used for outside lanterns or parasols, and was applied to the entire surface. The decoration is frugal but holds a surprise, since the colour of these marks gradually darkens with time.

Sensu, ogi, uchiwa: the fan

Of all the objects from bygone days, the fan is the one which has best stood the test of time. The businessman at the office, the sportsman after a workout, the tradesman behind his counter or the woman on the tube platform all use the fan in everyday life. The air-conditioner may have taken the place of the Gifu lantern, but it has not superseded the fan, which serves both as an accessory with which to fan oneself and as a symbol of good upbringing.

Opening a folding fan is a social act which links respect, a desire for happiness and the aesthetics of a thousand year old gesture. A number of crafted objects have been replaced by modern equivalents, but the memory of an entire people, in which the fan has a prominent position, lives on.

Like all paper objects, the fan comes from China. The very first were offered in homage by the princes of Korea, and from the 6th century onwards they appeared in the form of a circular frame over which paper or silk was stretched, like the skin of a drum. On this the Japanese based their own flat fan, the *uchiwa*, from the Heian period onwards. Its shape was finally fixed in the 14th century. A bamboo rod was split into many ribs at a node. Sheets of paper were then glued onto either side of this structure and fixed to an arc inserted at the base of the ribs. The "open" edge was simply covered by a ribbon folded in two. Numerous variations came into being in the 17th century, with the development of exchanges between regions. Already the military were using the commanding *gunbai*, in leather or lacquered paper, and ordinary people had taken to fanning their fires at home with a fan waterproofed with persimmon juice or lacquer. New developments were concerned with shape rather than with technical innovation – ovals, squares and full moons. The fans generally had 64 ribs or, more rarely, 45 or 80.

The development of the *uchiwa* began accelerate as soon as it became an object of artistic treatment. The Edo period was a peaceful time which allowed the expression of a rediscovered insouciance, and the *uchiwa* bore witness to this new style of living. It was decorated with painted designs which elevated it into the world of applied arts. In the summer, beautiful ladies in cotton *kimonos* carried such fans decorated by

Opposite:
Summer *uchiwa* fan

The flat fan is worn only with a cotton kimono, and is slipped into the belt when not in use.

Uchiwa

Kitchen uchiwa, *made from waterproof, lacquered paper.*

fashionable artists. The most famous of them, Korin (1661-1716), even created a type of fan which had 120 fine lacquered ribs and bore his name. Soon, the *uchiwa* became an essential publicity medium for theatrical actors, *sumo* wrestlers and famous courtesans. The great print artists were naturally enthusiastic about this new medium, and clothes-conscious women wasted no time in ruining themselves so they could own these artists' works. The *uchiwas* was so fashionable that at the end of the 19th century Masujiro Omura, a rebellious overlord, used one to direct a battle instead of the traditional war *gunbai*. Even today, the *maiko* and the *geisha* use fans inscribed with their name and the coat of arms of their house as visiting cards. They are heavily used in advertising, even though this is far removed from the aesthetic canons of tradition, and anyone can send a mini fan-shaped postcard.

The Chinese *uchiwa* became Japanese in spirit while retaining its original form. Like the parasol, another kind of fan was to become the very ideal of Japanese aesthetics by virtue of the specific nature of Japanese paper. This was the *sensu*, the folding fan. At the end of the 8th century it was nothing more than an assembly of superimposed cypress strips. It was later also made of sandalwood or Japanese cedar, before becoming popular in the form of an assembly of bamboo strips and folded paper. Its design was then so revolutionary that priests immediately conferred upon it a sacred function. Its pure form has the most divine simplicity. The accordion-shaped pleats, consisting of "mountain" and "valley" folds, are a reflection of Japan's own mountainous terrain. This thought probably occurred to a lady at of the 11th century court, who, after becoming a nun, dreamed of using the magical nature of the fan to treat the elder of the Mieido temple where she had chosen to live. The legend does not tell us whether it was the folded shape placed on the patient's forehead or the incantation recited by the nun which was the more effective, but following this cure, the technique of making folded paper into a fan was improved and so the true *sensu* came into being. Ribs were added to support and reinforce the fan's rigidity, and it was held together by a single rivet. Many workshops that specialised in the making of fans were named "Mieido" after this creation. Originally the *sensu* was reserved for communication with the gods, but its use became

Uchiwa

Fans for the Sumiyoshi-matsuri festival in Osaka.

extended to all prestigious occasions. Like the *gunbai* of the generals, it became a hierarchical symbol and was soon considered to be the ideal present for a superior. Moreover, its radiating shape, which some maintain was derived from the shape of a bat's wing, became in time a symbol of prosperity because of its spreading folds. It is for this reason that the *sensu* is a customary wedding present, and that the custom of giving folding fans as presents has become widespread. At New Year, a propitious time for gifts, the fans were made of the most beautiful white paper. In spite of their exceptional quality, these beautiful fans were easily damaged, so shopkeepers went back to their customers in mid-January to collect and repair them. Tradesmen also sold

Opposite and below:
Uchiwa

De luxe fans in openwork paper. Front and back.

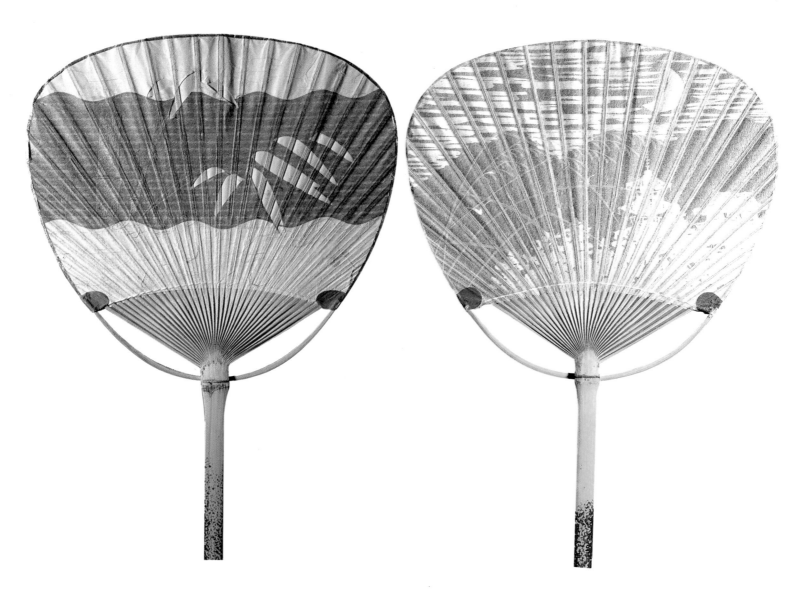

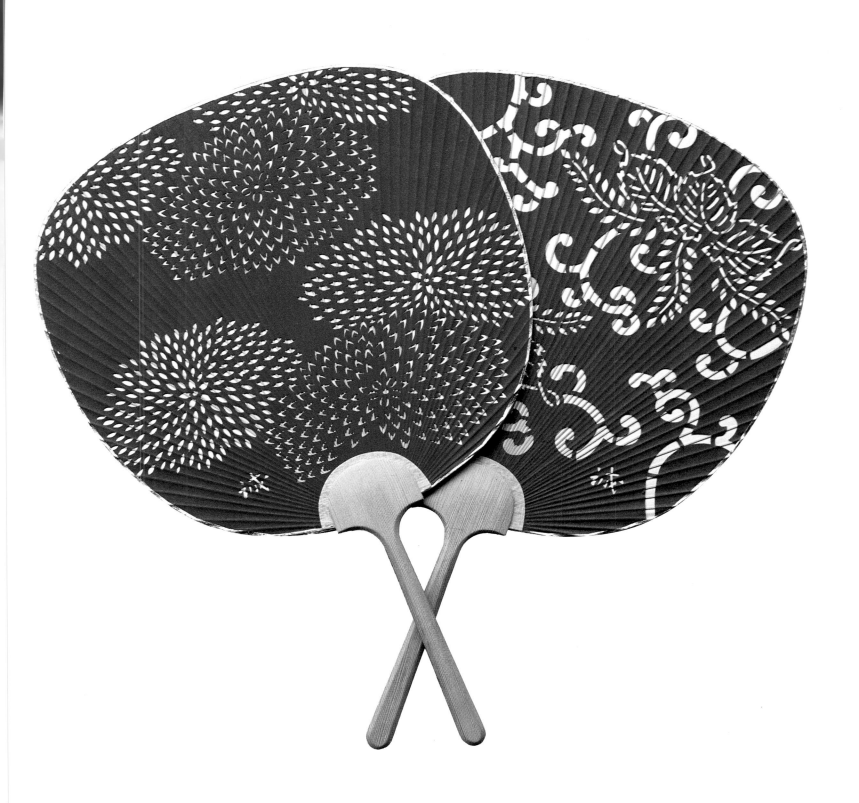

less prestigious fans, designed purely for fanning, with which they thoughtfully supplied spare sheets of pre-cut paper.

Just as they had done as for the parasol, the Japanese invented a thousand different uses for the fan, to which they gave corresponding names. From this large vocabulary, the term *ogi* was reserved for all fans which possessed a certain artistic value or had an aesthetic use. Their frames are usually perfectly cut and polished, and sometimes they are even lacquered or ornamented with openwork. This is the case with the stage fan which is used in dance and theatre, and also with the *chukei*, a very special shape of fan used to conduct ceremonies. This object, whose design dates from the Edo period, retains part of its radiating shape even when closed and is said to bring prosperity. Dance fans are generally heavy enough close to the rivet to allow a firmer grip, and are easy to open with a single flick of the wrist, whereas the "summer fan" must be made as light as possible so that it can be used without effort. Some fans are not necessarily made to be opened – this is true of the fan used in the tea ceremony, which is primarily a symbol of good upbringing and respect. It is carried before the guest when he enters the tea house, and is placed before him when he kneels. Used in all seasons, the tea fan cannot be considered as a means of obtaining cool air; rather, its religious nature comes to the fore as a symbolic barrier between the profane and sacred worlds. This function still persists even now at all ceremonial occasions, even though the fan no longer acts

Opposite and above:
Geisha uchiwa

The emblem of the House is painted on the front and the geisha's *name is written on the back.*

Making a *sensu*

Top:
The cut and glued fan shapes are placed in a press.
Centre:
Accordion pleating of precut sheets of paper.
Bottom:
A stick is slipped between the two sheets of paper which are stuck together.
Top right:
Brushing glue onto the ribs.
Bottom right:
Mounting the paper. The ribs are slipped between the two sheets of glued paper.
Opposite:
Sensu ribs.

Precut sheets of paper

Decorated sheets of paper ready for mounting.

Opposite:
Ogi

This fan, with calligraphy by an artist, is placed in the tokonoma of a home, where it joins works of art, incense burners, paintings and ikebana *bouquets in decorating this most noble alcove.*

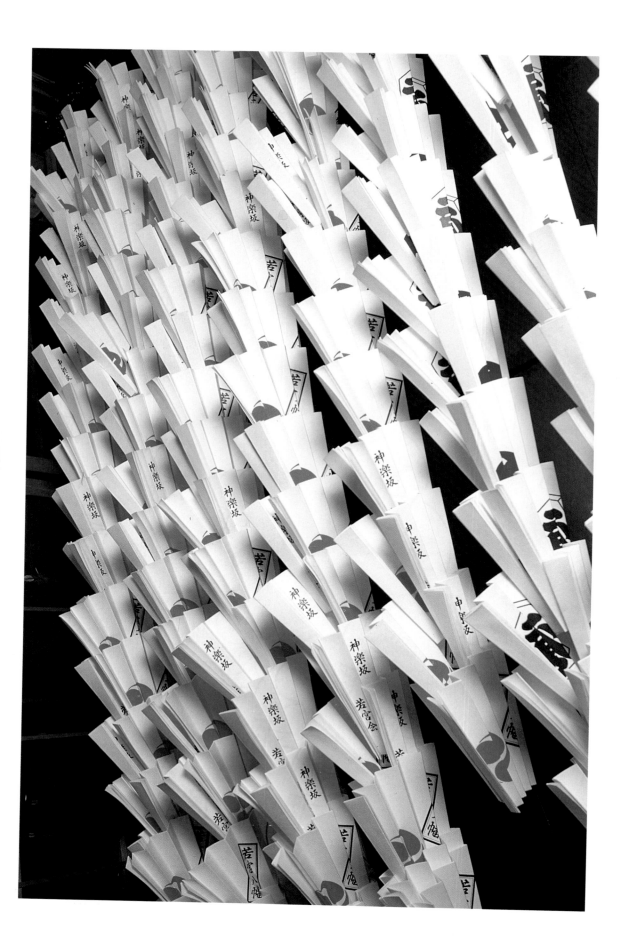

as an intermediary between the giver and the receiver, as it once did. From the Heian period onwards and throughout the Middle Ages, it was often used to present a missive to the emperor, important statesmen or clergy in acknowledgement of their sanctifying role. The habit of hiding a smile or an emotion behind a fan was probably derived from this custom; the expression of one's own personality was considered a "vulgar" thing which a well bred woman would refuse to impose on her entourage.

Thus, the Japanese fan is always the very epitome of quality: quality in its users, its gods and its craftsmen. Imported from China, it was very soon re-exported to its country of origin, and then from the 17th century onwards to Europe, where it became extremely popular. The Jesuits and Dutch sailors alike took fans home in their luggage and introduced these exotic proofs of their journey wherever they traded. Adorned with lace or peacock feathers, the *sensu* became universal.

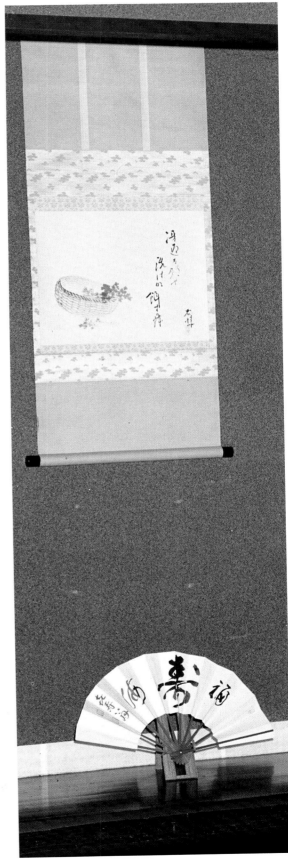

Dance *ogi*

Ceremonial *ogi*

Kabuki dance *ogi*

In the hands of a good actor, the fan can convey a wide range of emotions. Representation of nature, waves, clouds, flowers and birds is the theatre's way of placing the permanence of feelings within the great rhythm of the universe.

Geisha dance *ogi*

Each year, in the Spring, geisha girls from the "Houses" in Kyoto assemble for the dance spectacle called Miyako Odori. A typical element of Japanese hand movements, the fan has the place of honour in the dance.

Chigo

A sacred page at the Gion Festival in Kyoto. He carries the fan for the chukei ceremony on his back.

Opposite:
Three fans

Gold, silver and war fan. The latter is in oiled paper. The external frame is metal, to ward off sword blows.

Wagasa, the parasol

The parasol came to Japan from China in the 6th century and was originally a kind of silk-covered canopy. In about the 8th century another sort of parasol was developed which had a bamboo framework covered with paper. This object was used to protect the high clergy from the sun during ceremonies held outside the temple. From that time on, *shinto* considered the parasol to be the temporary residence of a deity, and it was soon also used by members of the aristocracy as a symbol of their dignity. The formal function of this parasol was expressed by the colour red, the symbol of ceremony. This aspect is still present in the tea ceremony as the places devoted to it are always marked by the presence of a large red parasol. Little by little, monks of a lower order themselves took shelter under small parasols, a custom which rapidly spread among the people, replacing the broad-brimmed hat which was used for protection against the rain and sun. These parasols were still very rustic and were usually made of plain oiled paper.

The superb craftsmanship of the refined Japanese parasol, *wa-gasa*, dates from the early years of the Edo period. The largest paper-making centres, situated in regions abundant in bamboo, specialised in making them. The most important centres were at Gifu, which supplied Kyoto, and at Fukui, where the annual production of 200,000 parasols was sent to the North of Japan. During this period, other centres began to assemble parasols, with paper often being imported from other regions. Japanese parasol paper from Fukui thus supplied some of the Edo workshops.

Until the Second World War, each province used its own combinations of colours, and makers had to be scrupulously careful not to confuse them. At this time, there were about 10,000 specialist craftsmen in Japan, but today this skill is disappearing due to competition from the Western umbrella industry since the 1950s.

Today, two main types of parasol survive: the *ban-gasa* and the *janome-gasa*. The term *ban-gasa* dates from the Edo period when shopkeepers inscribed a number (*ban*) on parasols lent to their customers on rainy days. The rather simple designs of the *ban-gasa* were suited to men, while the more elegant *janome-gasa* was the favourite of *kimono*-clad ladies. The latter's name derives from the special pattern with

Janome-gasa

Opposite:
Tea house

A parasol showing a place consecrated to the tea ceremony. These large parasols have rounded edges remiscent of old-fashioned parasols, on which gauze veils were attached to hide certain key figures from the gaze of the people.

Production

Top:
*Positioning the
perimeter ribs.*
Bottom:
*Positioning the paper
strips on the
circumference.*

which it was decorated: concentric or spiral, it stood out against a dark background and resembled a "snake's eye" (*ja-no-me*).

There are twelve stages in the production of a parasol.

The bamboo handle is attached to a small notched turret which takes the ribs, also made of bamboo. These ribs, which have holes in them, are linked together by strong cotton threads or by horsehair before being arranged in a regular fan shape. A thread is then fixed onto the free ends to keep them equidistant from one another.

Next, a ribbon folded in two is glued to the previously attached threads in order to form the perimeter of the parasol. This more solid edging provides a base for the triangular strips covering the ribs of the parasol (about fifty for men's parasols, forty for women's, and about one hundred for certain luxury parasols). This paper has to be strong and able to withstand the stress of glueing. It is generally a *kozo* paper, treated with persimmon juice. The craftsman must take special care to position it close to the turret so that water cannot enter. To this end, the peak of the parasol is reinforced by small paper triangles, adjusted every three ribs. This top piece is then hammered for a better finish. The parasol is moistened and left overnight.

The next day, the ribs are lacquered with a red mixture and the paper is dipped in flax or sesame oil. The master craftsman's assistants check the opening mechanism, which is decorated with a complex net of coloured threads, before handing the parasol over to the lacquer craftsman who will finish off the ribs. If the weather is not too uncertain, he will then arrange the parasols in a field to allow them to dry naturally before returning them to the workshop for final inspection.

A parasol made in this way should last for at least ten years, provided that it is used regularly to keep the paper in shape. As the paper becomes softer with humidity and contracts in the wind, it must be dried carefully after rain.

Made of bamboo and paper, the parasol remains a living object. Its admirers claim that it even communicates with them, and they never cease to praise the soft warmth of the handle in their hand, the sound of rain on the paper, the slight smell of lacquer and oil and, in particular, the delicacy of the light filtered through the paper and brought to life by its designs. Women also describe the harmony of its colours with that of their *kimono*. The Japanese parasol's divine aura, which lead to its initial religious use, still moves those who love the beauty and serenity that it radiates.

"Torn parasol"

It is thought that a torn parasol always hides a soul among its ribs.

Top:
Production

Gluing the strips.

**Young woman
arranging her hair**

Overleaf:
Field of parasols

*Parasols drying after
lacquering.*

Geisha show

*Dance parasols are
generally made of silk
so as to be transparent.*

White parasol

*Priests from the great
shrine of Ise carrying
the white parasol of
purity.*

Above and opposite:
**Umbrellas and
parasol of the
shinto procession**

*In many cases, the
parasol is considered as
the centre of the
cosmos.*

Paper games

Tako

*The eyes make a noise
when the kite is flying.*

Opposite:
Competition *tako*

Games, festivals and competitions have always been highly favoured by Japanese deities. Dance appeases them, the desire to win gratifies them and games of chance delight them. The early deities played, danced and sang to entice the Sun Goddess from her dark retreat. They innocently added a playful element to this important and solemn act. It is no surprise that they delight in games in which a personal appeal is made to them, such as the drawing out of oracles, or in games which represent them, like *sumo* wrestling. Many of these games were invented by men to please their divine creators, and so were very solemn, but over time they evolved for the simple purpose of amusement. Unwittingly, these games drew closer to their majestic models. Thus the kite, the doll, folded shapes and masks, which were originally designed to communicate with the celestial world, instead became ways of entertaining men as well as their gods.

Tako, the kite

The kite originated in China over 2000 years ago, and arrived in Japan relatively late, in the Heian period. Like most paper objects, it formed part of the religious act from the outset. The kite is often mentioned in Buddhist scripture, and *shinto* followers probably saw it as a kind of intermediary between heaven and earth. Following the Chinese example, the Japanese seem to have used it in the mediaeval period to place themselves physically above the common run of mor-

Yoshikawa
workshop at Kochi

For four generations, this workshop has been carrying on the tradition of the Tosa tako. The drawing is executed in Indian ink before being enhanced with bright colours in a rice glue base.

**_Tako_-hachi
workshop at
Shizuoka**

_Each region has its
repertoire of legendary
heroes. This workshop
only produces eight
models, hence its name
of "eight kites"._

**_Tako_ in the shape
of a spearhead**

*This type of kite, in
the shape of a
spearhead, was
intended exclusively
for samurai. The
motifs on this* tongari
*from Shizuoka are the
symbols of longevity
and health for the first
born son of a family.*

tals, although their aims may have been more profane; it was probably more a case of hoisting spies into the air with the aid of a paper sail. However, the *tako*, or kite, came into its own as a game.

It became very popular in the Edo period during the long winter months, when children competed with the wind in their liveliness. They looked forward to New Year's Day when they could fly the *tako* while their parents celebrated the more serious rites connected with the changing of the year. In the 17th and 18th centuries, adults could no longer resist the pleasure of pitting themselves against their offspring. *Tako* battles were a great release in peacetime, channelling the citizens' energy and sharpening the competitive spirit of village societies. Kites increased in size in order to prove the strength of their handlers. At Nagasaki and Hamamatsu, traditional sites for large scale encounters, it is not uncommon to fly sails of between three and six square metres, each one needing between thirty and forty people to operate it and a group leader to coordinate the manoeuvre. Each year, aeronautical experts take part in these demonstrations and attempt to fly increasingly larger structures which require the efforts of dozens of "market porters" – a tonne of traction for the most gigantic. In this respect they follow the tradition of the Tokushima *wan-wan*, some of which measured up to twenty-eight metres in diameter and required thousands of sheets of paper to make. However, the main purpose of the kite remains that of aerial combat, and the size of the object has little real importance in relation to the skill of the team of flyers. The strings are coated with glass powder or fitted with razor blades to cut their adversary's string or its stabilising tail. These tails, which are beautifully decorated, also make noises which punctuate the antics of the *tako*. They were usually very long and help to identify the teams since each region has its own motifs and colours. They are also very useful for manoeuvring the tiny tako, scarcely bigger than a postcard, which older people, proud of their long years of practice, master to perfection, watched by their grandchildren.

Centipede kite

The most difficult to handle.

Kite

*Some kites are real
graphic works of art by
print experts.*

**Tako with
ideogram motif**

*A speciality of the
Izumo prefecture.
They are always flown
in pairs: the "tortoise"
ideogram (black) on
the left; the "crane"
ideogram (red) on the
right. The kite in the
shape of a turnip
originates from
Takamatsu and the
kite in the shape of a
lantern is typical of the
island of Shikoku.*

Overleaf:
**Tako in the shape
of a fan with
dragon motif**

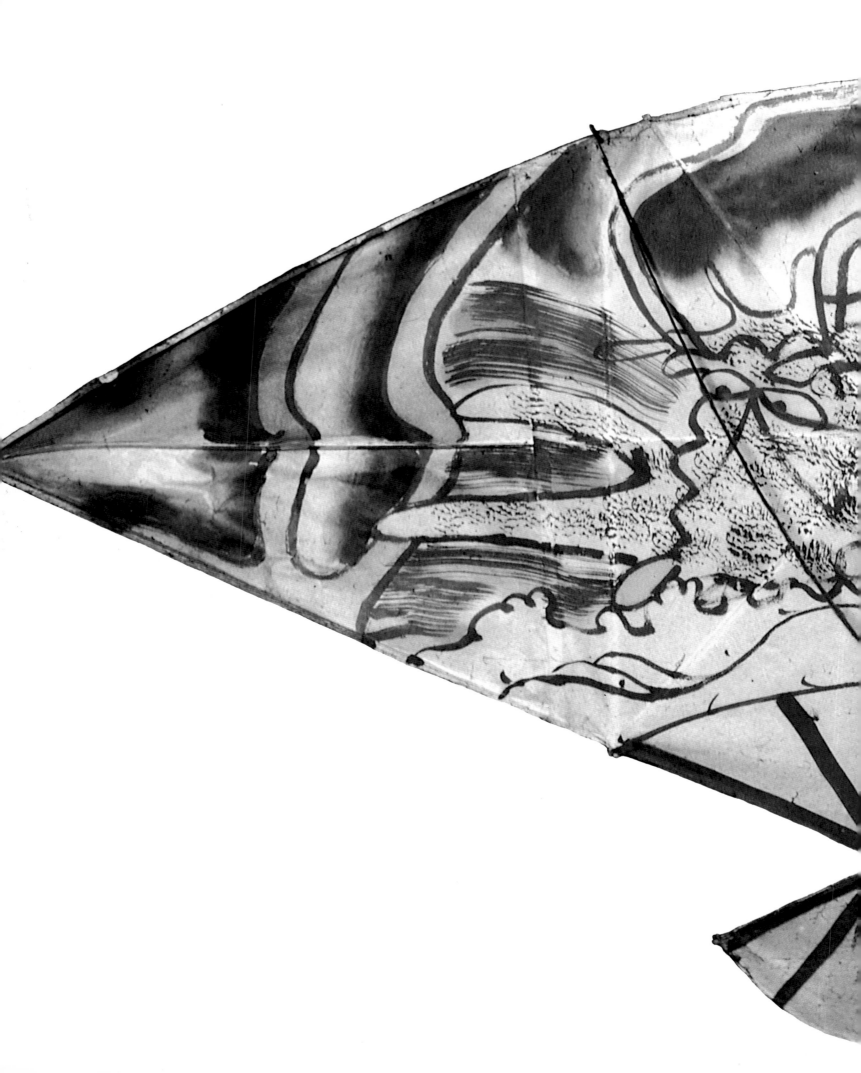

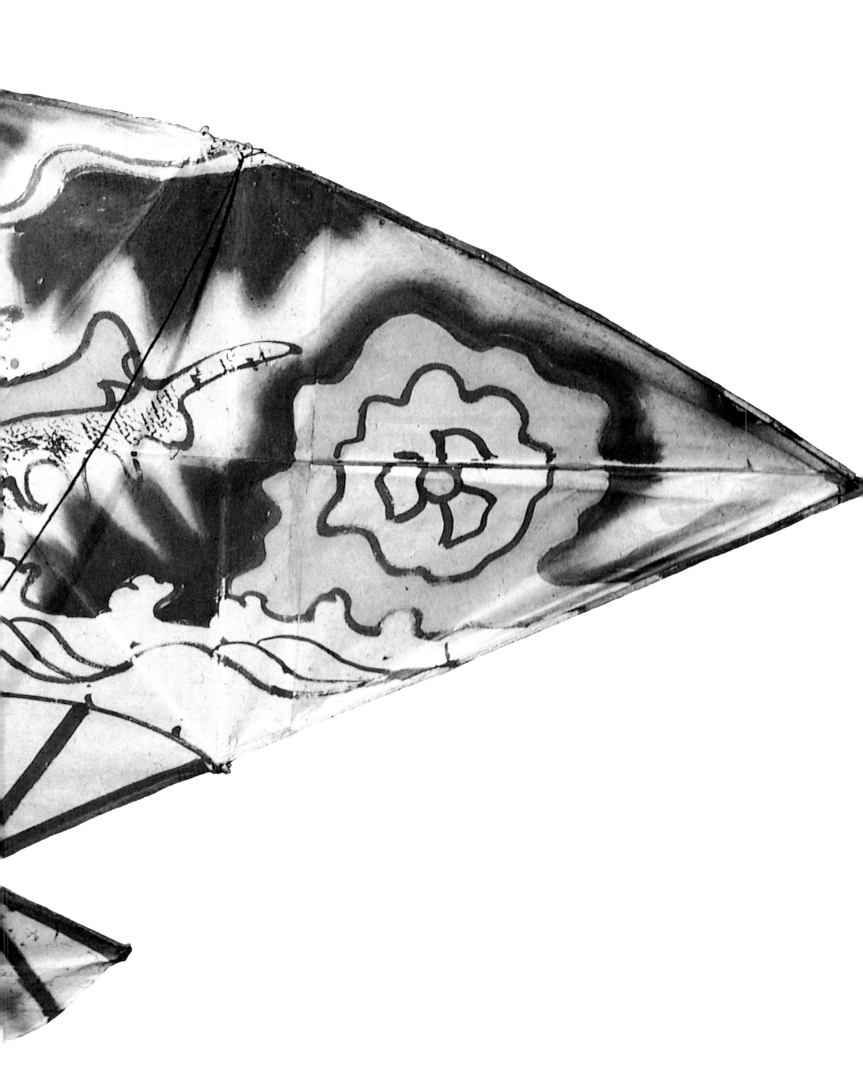

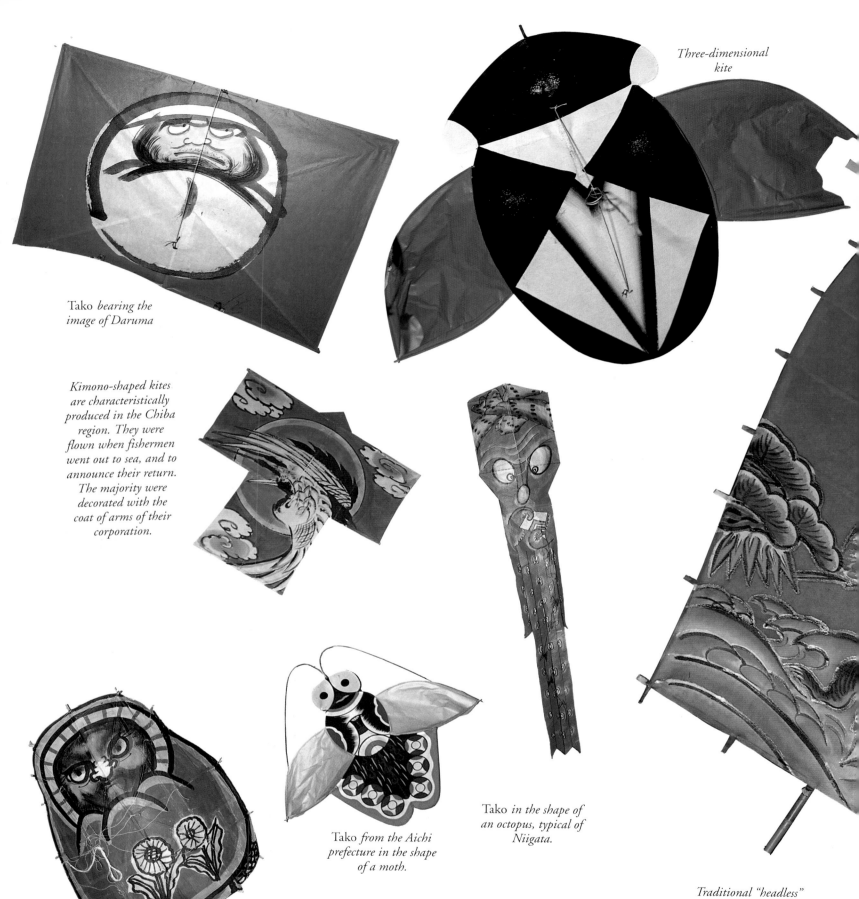

Tako *bearing the image of Daruma*

Three-dimensional kite

Kimono-shaped kites are characteristically produced in the Chiba region. They were flown when fishermen went out to sea, and to announce their return. The majority were decorated with the coat of arms of their corporation.

Tako *in the shape of Daruma*

Tako *from the Aichi prefecture in the shape of a moth.*

Tako *in the shape of an octopus, typical of Niigata.*

Traditional "headless" tako *from Shizuoka, showing the crane and the tortoise, symbols of longevity.*

132

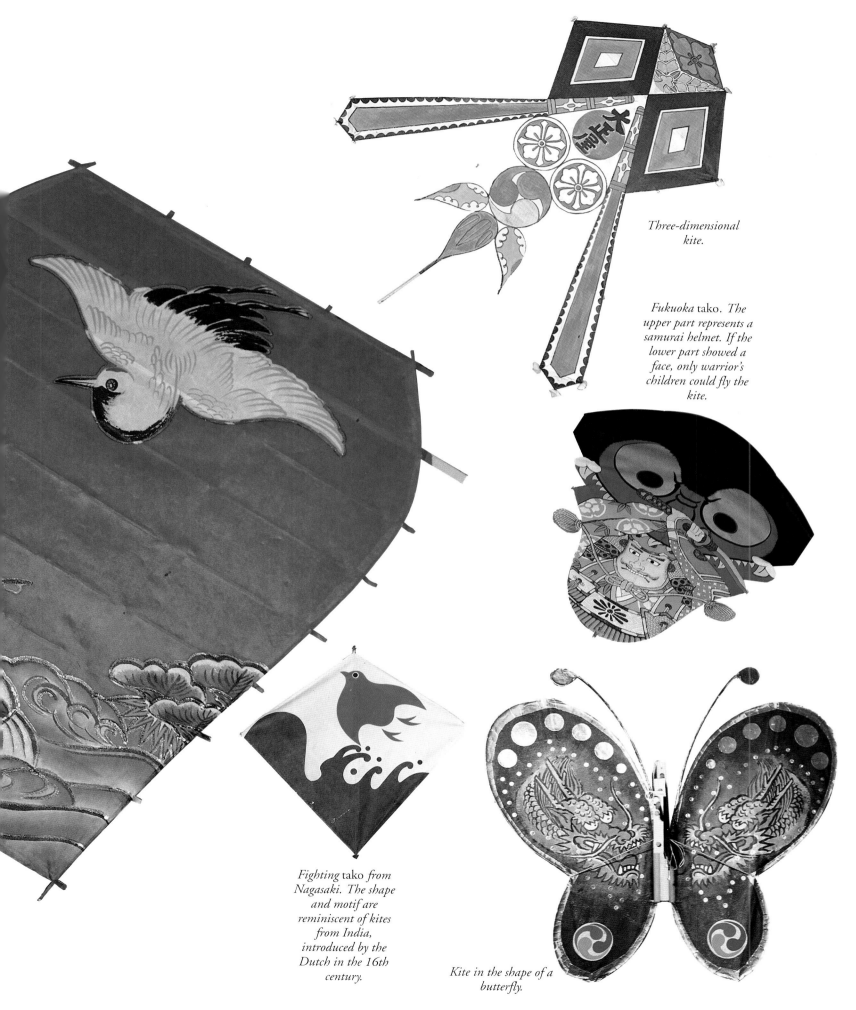

Three-dimensional kite.

Fukuoka tako. *The upper part represents a samurai helmet. If the lower part showed a face, only warrior's children could fly the kite.*

Fighting tako *from Nagasaki. The shape and motif are reminiscent of kites from India, introduced by the Dutch in the 16th century.*

Kite in the shape of a butterfly.

133

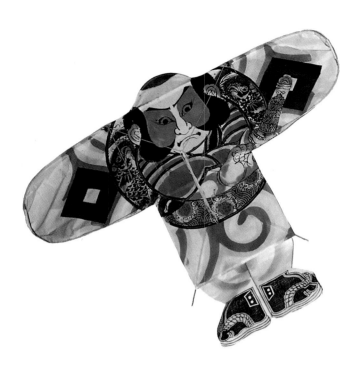

Kite shapes are many and varied. Through them, the regions promote their great men, fierce warriors and children of legend, when they are not simply using them to portray "characters" dear to every Japanese: the crane, the cicada, the octopus, the butterfly, the dragon, the servant (*yakko-san*), the hero Yoshitsune and his companion Benkei, Saint Daruma, the *kabuki* actor or the fashionable *geisha*. The basic repertoire is completed by the fan printed with the imperial sun, the coat of arms of a family or clan, and ideograms of good omen. The latter are very elaborately cut out, following the shape of the writing itself. The craftsman has to master the laws of balance and flight in order to combine correctly the bamboo ribs, paper strips and support strings. However, the most widespread form of the *tako* is a simple geometric paper polygon stretched over a frame, which derives its beauty from its single painted decoration, often executed by famous artists.

The ideal paper for *tako* making is kozo because of its strength and flexibility, but the exact composition of the pulp often remains a jealously guarded secret. The

Tako with sleeves

Kite from Edo *representing* yakko-san, *the servant. When dressed as a fireman, he promotes the idea of fire-fighting.*

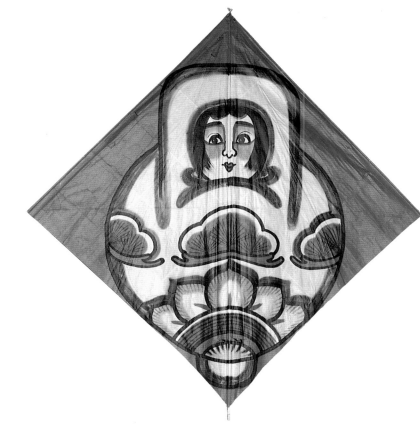

paper is not waterproofed, so its correct composition is especially important if the kite is to behave properly in both wet and dry weather. The decoration alone affords some protection to the kite's surface. If regional models are very numerous, those created by the tako craftsman are generally limited in number. Most craftsmen specialise in a particular range – the *Tako-hachi* workshop at Shizuoka only made eight models featuring popular heroes, hence its name *tako* (kite)-*hachi* (eight). The artist always starts by drawing the outline of the design directly onto the paper in black and white to suggest its graphic rhythm. Colour is then applied to add a liveliness consistent with this dynamic object. *Tako* craftsmen often also work in areas which use very similar designs, though these need not be on paper. This is the case with the long clan banners which are still used for historical processions or more frequently with *koi-nobori*, wind socks in the shape of a carp which are floated in the wind on the day of the boys' festival – the fifth day of the fifth month. Up until the 19th century these carp were all made of paper.

Large fighting *tako*

Kochi region.

Centre:
Kite

It represents Tenjin, the kami *of calligraphy. Aichi prefecture.*

Hariko, papier-mâché heroes

Papier-mâché was greatly valued from the Nara period onwards for making small Buddhist sculptures. It was designed to be lacquered, but was never serious competition for carved wood or dry lacquer statues. One single papier-mâché work has come down through the centuries and deserves to figure in the pantheon of major creations. It is the Monjubosatsu statue, preserved since 1269 at the temple of Chuguji. This technique only truly developed with the birth of popular art in the Edo period. It was encouraged by the eighth Tokugawa *shogun*, Yoshimune (1677-1751). This exceptional man, an astute and dutiful politician, had all the frugality of his ancestral warriors. He passed numerous laws intended to check the aesthetic excesses which had overtaken society, from overlords to simple citizens. Under these restrictions, toy makers had to stop using very costly materials and excessively "princely" effects. *Hariko*, papier-mâché, took the place of fine porcelain, rare wood and precious lacquers. Recycled paper found a lasting future. It was light and cheap, and it had the advantage that it could be modelled at will and would harden on drying. Also, it was easy to duplicate models so ensuring a wide public distribution.

Thanks to paper, the heroes of popular belief could thus be adopted by all families for the protection of their members. Among these, the papier-mâché dog, *inu-hariko*, is still very popular. He is offered to the newborn male child at his presentation at the shrine in order to protect him from evil influences and to allow him to acquire wealth and honour. The association between the dog and religion goes back to the 4th century when Kobo-daishi, founder of the *shingon* Buddhist sect, caused a real dog to be born from a simple design on a paper talisman in order to thank a peasant for his hospitality. The latter needed help in fighting bears which were terrorising the region. Much later, under the government of Tokugawa Tsunayoshi, man became the protector of dogs. This *shogun* was in despair because he had no descendants. A monk told him that this misfortune was the just punishment for a former life in which he had shown no respect for living things. The *shogun* then decreed that the killing of animals was to be prohibited throughout the land. As this declaration took effect in 1687, the Year of the Dog in

Warrior's mask

Opposite:
From paper to papier-mâché

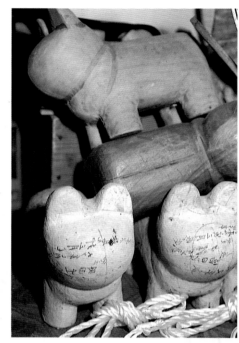

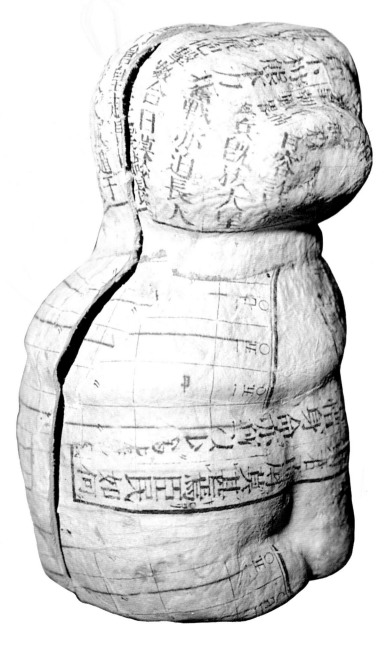

Production

Top, from left to right:
Sheet of recycled washi
to make hariko.
Wooden mould.
*Paper plastered down on
the mould.*
Centre:
Mould and finished
hariko.
Bottom left:
Inu-hariko *from
Shizuoka.*
Bottom right:
Hariko *split for removal
from mould.*

A cat calling
upon wealth

Votive plaque

Votive plaque in the shape of a fox.

the zodiacal calendar, dogs were the first beneficiaries of the new law, and the old and the sick among them could end their days in a refuge built on the shogun's orders. At that time, the famous writer Bakin wrote the *Story of Eight Faithful Dogs*, which enjoyed considerable success. The inu-hariko models vary from one region to another. In Tokyo, the dog carries a tambourine on his back and allows a baby to play with it while he keeps watch. At Shizuoka, he carries a fan, the symbol of prosperity. In some cases, he wears a sheet of paper glued to his muzzle, symbolising the prevention of all respiratory illness. In others, he wears a rope like the ones on which old coins used to be threaded, indicating a wish for wealth. The most common accessory in Tokyo models is the basket, which covers the dog's head completely like an oversized hat. It simply represents the innocent games of the puppy at home, and the gods appreciate it above all others for its *joie de vivre*. Before the war, as many as 200 different models of *inu-hariko* could be found. The most important regions of production were: Toyoka (Aichi prefecture), Tokyo, Tokoishi (Hiroshima), Takamatsu (Shizuoka), Fushimi (Kyoto), Kume (Okayama), Tosa (Kochi) and Katsumata (Hyogo).

The *inu-hariko* maker did not confine himself to this model alone. Each new year a new animal in the Chinese zodiac was protected. A series of twelve animals was therefore fashioned by craftsmen: the rat, cow, tiger, hare, dragon, snake, horse, sheep, monkey, cockerel, dog and wild boar. Some of them are particularly noteworthy because they are supposed to have special powers. The "red cow" is venerated in the North in memory of the cattle which transported building materials for a local temple. One of them in particular refused to leave the site when the work was finished. This fact would have been forgotten had a smallpox epidemic not broken out at that very time. It was later realised that children who owned a *hariko* of this red cow were saved, whereupon its effigy naturally became an amulet against smallpox.

The tiger became equally famous. As an animal it was unknown in Japan, but it accompanied generals into battle in a decorative and symbolic form since its tail ornamented the sheaths of their swords. It was appreciated all the more in the Kumamoto region when the famous Kato Kiyomasa, on a campaign in Korea, single-handedly slew a fearsome tiger, the symbol of

Mask of Okame

Right and opposite:
**Masks of Okame
and Hyottoko**

*The two typical masks
of agricultural society
which were worn for
comic dances: the
woman, Okame,
symbolises wealth; the
man, Hyottoko, is the
spirit which protects
against fires.*

Hariko

From top to bottom:

Tumbling dolls.

Servant and Daruma.

Daruma on an ox with a nodding head.

The association of the ox and the saint is very common in Buddhism as the monks in search of truth often sat astride an ox in the Chinese countryside.

Hariko *of a hare.*

Hariko *of a goat.*

Hariko

From top to bottom:

Hariko *of a tiger.*

Fox mask.

*Cat calling
upon wealth.*

お亀　　　河童　　　山姥　　　小

御河童　　　行火　　　丹下左膳　　　福禄寿

付目　　　竹庵　　　鬼祭司　　　半四

布袋

火吹き

奴

鬼大将

笠地蔵

Masks of idiots

147

**Hariko in the shape
of fish**

Hariko *moulded in
the shape of fish,
arranged head to head.
The fins and tails are
added later.*

Korean power. In the Edo period, it became an assistant to the police when it became the custom for magistrates to sit between three and five o'clock, the zodiacal hour of the tiger. It was often drawn on the folding screens or partitions of official buildings to express fear of justice.

The Japanese have a particular affection for the hare. It is gentle in appearance and is loved by children who look for it on nights when the moon is full. For, while we in the West see a Man in the Moon, in Japan people believe they can see a rabbit plundering the rice.

The dragon is the fifth animal of the cycle. The perfect embodiment of duality, it links heaven and earth, fire and water. The Chinese defined its form: a snake's body, a horse's head, a deer's antlers, a demon's eyes, a cow's ears, a carp's fins, a tiger's feet and an eagle's claws. It is difficult to be more eclectic in the animal kingdom – this is perhaps the secret of its unchallenged success.

The monkey is certainly the most venerated animal. Its comical appearance makes it special, but above all it personifies the year of wealth in the zodiac. It is also often associated with the god of the highway and, by extension, with people such as tumblers who "work the roads". As a reminder of these travelling companions it often carries a tambourine, but the red shorts it usually wears have a another significance. They are said to avert smallpox, and for this reason the monkey is often given to children. As for its warrior's headdress, this hints at power. The "climbing monkey" figurines which are a speciality of Miyazaki display all these attributes. In these, the papier-mâché monkey is shown clinging to a pole which bears the standard of the Boys' Festival, decorated with irises. When the pole sways, the animal climbs to the top.

Hariko include various other lucky charms which do not necessarily belong to the zodiac, such as Saint Daruma, whom we have mentioned already, and *maneki-neko*, the cat. In Japan, the cat won the acclaim always denied it by the zodiac because it was the only animal which did not weep over the death of Buddha, being too busy at the time hunting for mice. Curiously, it is this quality for which the cat is appreciated in Japan, and particularly so in the temples where sacred texts appear to be highly prized by the rats. However, its consecration came about not because of its services to religion, but because of a love story. Long ago in

Tiger

Tiger with nodding head, a speciality of the Shimane prefecture.

"Climbing monkey"

A speciality of Miyazaki. Generally, the pole ends in a standard, but in this variation, the monkey mounts an assault on a dragonfly.

Edo, there were two tea houses which used porcelain cats to attract customers. The house to the East of the Eko-in temple had a golden cat, while the house to the West had a silver cat. The owner of the first fell into debauchery, but his wife compensated for her husband's incompetence with her smiling welcome. One of her customers fell in love with her. The beautiful woman did not resist his advances for long, and extracted large sums of money from him. Ruined and in debt, the poor unfortunate man was considering expiating his conduct, when his repentant mistress suggested that she would join him in Death. Their double suicide caused a sensation in Edo and their story became so famous that the tea house with the golden cat eclipsed its rival, which had to close down. From that time on, the "calling cat" lucky charm became a part of the folklore of restaurants and shops, and it occupies a place of honour on the family alters of the *demi-monde*.

Economical to make, the *hariko* requires very thick recycled paper which is applied to a mould made of hard, insect-resistant wood. To be sufficiently supple, the paper must be soaked in water for about twenty days. Complicated models often require longer. The figure thus obtained is split in two so that it can be taken off the mould, and is then glued back together. Strips of old, thin paper are then stuck onto the model to ensure a good finish. Once dry, the model is painted to give character and life to the figure.

Children seek to take on this life and character when they dress up as their heroes. More seriously, the ancient Japanese believed that it was possible to enter the world of the gods by wearing a mask. This is why masks and make-up are so prevalent in the theatre and in religious processions, which are derived from the theatre. *Hariko* caricatures which are carried by children combine the dual advantage of mask and make-up, as they are often brightly coloured. Comic characters, either crafty or drunk, from the seedy districts are evidently those preferred by boisterous children.

Origami, the art of folding

With the mastery of its production and the invention of recycling, paper spread and penetrated the homes of the *samurai* as much as it had the palaces and shrines.

Miharu dolls

Fukushima prefecture. These papier-mâché characters are among the most sophisticated in Japan.

151

During the 14th century, housewives began to improve the presentation of certain domestic products and the "packaging" of various household utensils. They folded paper in which to keep powdered medicines, medicinal plants and strips of dried fish. They also used paper to seal jars. It was not long before this kind of utilitarian paper folding was enriched by subtle decoration, and *origami* became one of the subjects studied by well-educated girls. Pre-folded sheets of paper for origami were already available in the 18th century.

It is an aesthetic extension of the use of sachets, envelopes and paper cones to wrap in them traditional presents of thread, needles, make-up powders, chopsticks, fans or combs, endowing them with the sacred quality appropiate to gifts between civilised people. Thus in 1728 there was a trade in "boxes with five hundred folds", the models being practical, ceremonial or playful in nature.

Very early on, the Japanese felt the need to compile a list of the basic *origami* shapes. Three major books on the subject have come down to us: *Sembazuru-origata* and *Chushingura-origata*, both dating from 1797, and *Kan-no-mado*, compiled about 1850. This last brings together documents apparently going back to the year 1000, the era when paper folding became established as a social art. It is not surprising to see religious and ceremonial folded forms taking pride of place, but we must also mention the folding of shapes for pleasure. Many *origami* models in this last category make playful reference to a symbolism charged with superstition.

Kan-no-mado means "Window for the cold season", a rather impenetrable title even for contemporary Japanese. Its most probable interpretation is "Practical and poetic studies to occupy winter evenings", a good way of fighting winter melancholy. The author, Katsuyuki Adachi, points out that paper folding is an aristocratic pastime. One of the five volumes is entirely devoted to paper folding. It consists of six pages of text, five pages of ceremonial folded shapes from the Ogasawara school and fifty-one pages of playful *origami*, the most simple of them being shown with an explanatory diagram. The models are mostly those which have become classics in the West: the dragonfly, the crane, the monkey, the persimmon, the aubergine, the wild boar, the cicada, the snail, the crab, the iris, the shrimp, the frog, the boat and the lotus bud. Some of them can only be identified by the Japanese, like the *shinto* table

Opposite:
Panda

Making shapes geometrical is the basic technique of paper folding.

Traditional crab

One of the three classic folded shapes from the year 1000. The legs were made of cut-out shapes.

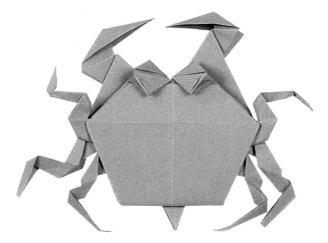

Child with *origami*

The tradition of the fold also exists in clothing. Since the 18th century, the girls' kimono belt has lent itself to many representational variations.

for offerings, the aristocrats' chariot, the *sumo* arena or the portrait of the Six Poets. The folded shapes from this period may have notches or cuts in them such as those practised in *shinto*, but great importance is not attached to sculpture except in the rare models like the crab, the octopus or the monkey. The paper formats vary depending on the object to be folded; the dragonfly needs a regular hexagon, the monkey, with its long arms, needs an irregular polygon, but the majority of subjects can be made from a simple basic square. The Japanese have always loved classifying the most beautiful manifestations of their culture. In terms of folded shapes, the *Three Origami* are the crane, the frog and the crab. The folded shape of the crane, with its slender delicacy, comes closest to Japanese aesthetics. The frog is more plastic due to the skill of its geometrical form. The crab is the most complex with its six legs and two pincers. All these models date from 1000 ad, even if, in the course of history, they have undergone some modifications and improvements in the intervening years.

The folded shapes of *Chushingura-origata* represent the characters of a play which relates the eventful life of the forty-seven faithful. These men were obliged to disembowel themselves for having avenged their outraged overlord by killing his offender. The folded shapes reconstruct the very special atmosphere of this popular theatre, with its studied scenes, aesthetic poses and exaggeratedly shaped costumes. These compositions were doubtlessly based on prints representing famous actors of the 18th century which were then in vogue.

The very idea of transformation and rapid change of appearance on stage is also akin to paper folding, where the subject often only appears at the last moment, thus creating the most theatrical of surprises. The twenty five characters presented in folded form are all variations on the same basic principle. Whether seated or standing, they are made of paper cut to form arms and legs. The eyes, mouth and hairstyle are painted onto each *origami* figure.

The author of the book in question also wrote *Sembazuru-origata*. Some claim that he was a superior at a hermitage in the Ise region. Others think he was a poet writing under the pseudonym of a lady at court, for there are poems accompanying each plate of folded forms. Still others believe that the two people

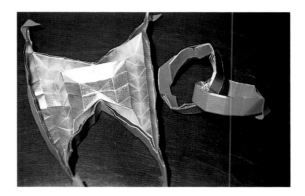

Contemporary *origami*

Film or cartoon characters feature more and more frequently in the repertoire of folded shapes.

Below:
Folded shapes based on geometry and mathematical volume are very common today. Many contemporary people working with folded shapes also belong to the scientific world. On the right, rings interlaced without any cuts. On the left, the same origami unfolded.

**Fruit salad
in a dish**

*Representational
productions composed
of several folded shapes
are star attractions at*
origami *exhibitions.*

Traditional frogs

*One of the classic
folded shapes, and the
oldest one that can be
altered by being
expanded.*

**Hiroshima
memorial**

*Dedicated to the
young Sadako Sasaki,
a victim of atomic
radiation.*

collaborated to write this major work. The title means "Folding of a thousand cranes". However, the work itself only shows forty-nine different *origami* models of cranes, each one bearing an individual name, but the number of possible variations is infinite. The figure "Thousand" in the title does not refer to the number of folded shapes, but to the tradition which believes that a crane lives for a thousand years. Particularly dear to the Japanese, the crane is the inspiration for feats of the kind achieved by a virtuoso in 1986 with a one millimetre square of paper, which he folded into a crane with the help of a needle and a microscope. More seriously, this very positive symbol always accompanies wishes for longevity and recovery from illness. After the Second World War, the crane also became an image of peace. The story behind this concerns a little girl, called Sadako Sasaki, who was a victim of the atomic radiation from Hiroshima. On her hospital bed, she folded cranes using paper from medicine sachets. She hoped that she would be cured if she folded a thousand cranes. As she worked at her folding, she remembered her unfortunate companions in her prayers. She folded 644 small white paper birds before she died. Many other Japanese children were moved to copy her actions in an attempt to perpetuate her desire for universal peace. In 1958, a monument was erected in the Memorial Park at Hiroshima. At its summit a bronze statuette depicts a little girl folding a crane. Multicoloured garlands of birds made by children all over the world have since kept Sadako's memorial company. It is this desire for hope which leads sympathetic people to lay this tiny paper object, which has become such a marvellous symbol, in front of all the memorial plaques and mausoleums at Hiroshima and Nagasaki.

The most extraordinary folded cranes are those made of several birds folded out of a single sheet. The sheet is then cut according to a precise drawing, so that the mother carries her little ones at the end of her beak, wings and tail. Entire garlands can be made in this way. The pair of cranes touching beaks is equally charming, and much easier to make.

According to these documents and others which are less complete, *origami* for amusement can be dated back to the year 1000, but it only really became popular in the Muromachi period (1333-1573) with the invention of about fifty new folded shapes without cuts. At the end of the Edo period, about seventy traditional playful

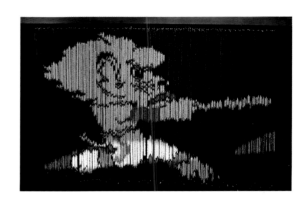

"The thousand cranes"

Origami of cranes made up to form a curtain symbolising the image of the victor at the Lions baseball club in Tokyo.

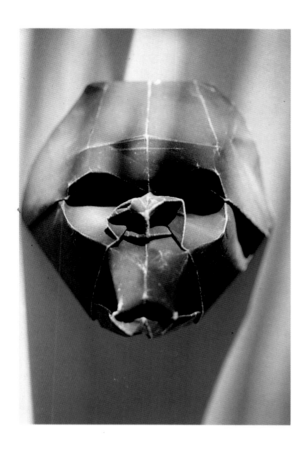

Origami by Akira Yoshizawa

Initiator of the artistic renewal of origami, the grand master of Japanese folded shapes primarily seeks representational authenticity.

origami were regularly made. Several decades later, during the reign of Emperor Meiji, many had already been forgotten, especially the old religious folded shapes. The symbols of the past were sold off to Westerners who were eager for exotica. The cranes, frogs, carps and cicadas lost their symbolic meaning and their sacred aura, to become no more than pure objects of amusement for children and women at home. It was in the reign of Emperor Taisho (1912-1926) that the use of square coloured paper became widespread and that *origami* became an integral part of teaching at girls' schools. This did not last for long, however, since during the following reign it lost its prestige in the eyes of educationalists, who considered it to be too formal and repetitive.

Only some *origami* artists keep traditional models alive, from which they draw the inspiration for their new creations. In 1941, the first *origami* manual was published. It showed complex forms composed of several folds, like the horse or the peacock. Under the impetus of masters like Akira Yoshizawa, the Japanese art of paper folding blossomed anew after the Second World War. Toshie Takahama, Isao Honda, Kosho and Mishio Uchiyama, Kunihiko Kasahara, Toyoaki Kawai and Yoshihide Momotani are some of the famous names. They all wanted to revitalise the creativity of *origami*, not only in their own country, but throughout the world, and they forged close ties with others skilled in the art of paper folding from every continent.

Japanese *washi* is ideal for folding. It can be manipulated ten times more often than the best Western paper. It resists the trial and error of beginners and folds obediently to the extravagances of accomplished creators. Depending on what the modeller plans to make, the paper needs to be thick or thin, smooth or textured, stiff or supple. All the creator asks is that it retains its fold lines, for once unfolded, it can serve as a reference for drawing its diagram. For the novice, this quality will help his understanding of the principles of overlapping and reversing folds and of how each creation takes shape. Western paper, which is less supple and elastic than *washi*, is however recommended for beginners making folded shapes with points. Japanese paper remains indispensable for folding complicated models like the "thousand cranes", where the slender link joining each bird is no more than one to five millimetres thick.

Gorilla by Akira Yoshizawa

This type of work requires a strong and highly resistant paper. The sculptured parts are moistened for better modelling.

No mask

The mask of the adulterous woman transforming herself into a demon is one of the most typical of the no theatre. The mask is one of the most creative ranges of contemporary folded shapes.

Heart upon lips

*Contemporary studied
elegance.*

Left and right:
Tato

Tato *are decorative
envelopes designed to
hold tiny objects like
needles or thread.
Larger, more sober
ones do exist to wrap
kimonos in.*

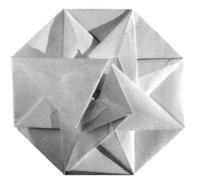

Cockerel by Isao Honda

This folded shape is made up of two origami *fitted together. It is based on a search for abstract rhythm typical of that practised by architectural students of the Bauhaus in Weimar during the 1920s.*

Previous page:
Tsuru

The "crane" is the perfect symbol of Japanese folded shapes, and one of the oldest.

But whatever the material, both Japanese and Westerners are in agreement with the master Yoshizawa: "An *origami* must be as simple and free of ornamentation as possible. If you have to paint or decorate it to make it comprehensible, it is no longer an *origami'*. In other words, the primary dictum of paper folding states that all you need is one sheet of paper, ten fingers, no glue or scissors or pencils, and a lot of imagination.

Dolls that are not made for play

At the start of spring on 3rd March, dolls take the place of honour for *Hina-matsuri*, the Festival of Dolls, which is celebrated on this day. It is a festival reserved for girls – boys have their own on 5th May. In 12th century rural Japan, the return of good weather was celebrated on this occasion, and people made preparations for agricultural work to begin. Everyone made rustic dolls from paper or straw and threw them into rivers to ward off misfortune and illness. From time immemorial, these protective charms have never been children's playthings in rural areas.

During the same period, noble families established the custom of decorating the house with a set of court dolls in the hope of ensuring the emperor's protection, as he was the descendant of the Sun Goddess. There were fifteen of these dolls: the Emperor and Empress, three ladies in waiting, five musicians, two ministers and three guards. In the centuries that followed, the dolls became increasingly luxurious, and the custom spread throughout all classes of society. On the eve of 3rd March, mothers and daughters busy themselves preparing the red dais for the imperial couple, as well as offerings for the gods and sweets for the neighbourhood children who are invited in.

The ceremony was perfected during the shogunate of Ienari (1773-1841), the father of many daughters. He wished to protect Japan from any foreign influence, and took a personal interest in establishing former imperial and feudal customs as features of Japanese life. While playing with dolls, little girls learned traditional women's skills from the older girls and women: the art of making bouquets, the tea ceremony and *origami*. In Edo working-class families, dolls were not as precious as those found in the Kyoto palace.

Aerodrome by Yoshihide Momotani

Left:
Balls and modular decorations

They were only made of paper, like the former effigies which were thrown into the river. Yet, for all that, they did not lack refinement. Hair made of crumpled paper carefully reproduced the hairstyles appropriate to each age-group, the *kimonos* made of coloured or printed paper matched one another in accordance with the aesthetic rules for clothing. The characters were made even more life-like by cuts made in the paper or by touches of paint indicating the eyes and mouth. They were looked on as treasures, and great care was taken not to let them fall into the destructive hands of tiny children. At the end of the Edo period, and particularly at the start of the Meiji period, the making of *ane-sama* dolls became a leisure activity for older people.

As with all popular crafts, each region had its own typical models, even if differences lay only in the most delicate nuances of shape and colour. At Shizuoka, Mrs Suzuki perpetuates the tradition of dolls created by her grandfather. Her mother and then her sister maintained the tradition of these faceless dolls, which are like mirrors onto which anyone can project his own personality. She remembers that as a child she played with them, but today they are merely displayed in a cabinet. They are always presented with their back to the viewer so that the amazing hairstyles of the past can be admired.

In general, these dolls have a cotton face covered with white paper, the hairstyles being sufficient to indicate the age or position of the individual. Mrs Tamura also designs the faces of her dolls in this way, but she adds the characteristic features of *kabuki* make-up to some of them. All these creations take their characters from the expressionism of this kind of theatre, and strive to recreate its atmosphere. The stylised poses, the exaggerated shapes of the costumes and the extensive repertoire of heroes make these dolls works of art which are comparable to porcelain and brocade items.

Many contemporary makers of dolls approach their work in a similar way. The thousand facets of Japanese paper and the equally numerous techniques employed in giving it expression have led to the birth of the art of the paper doll, relegating plastic figures to the world of children's toys.

Opposite:
Doll by Isako Tamura

Below:
Traditional paper doll

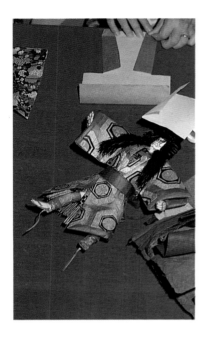

Production

Dolls made by Isako Tamura are all part of the kabuki *repertoire.*

Right:
Kabuki doll

Games of happiness

Kites, *hariko*, *origami* and dolls have become fundamental to Japanese culture through the ages. Their religious nature or more simply their typically Japanese design has always preserved them from the trivia of ordinary life, and it is only recently that they have entered the realm of play. However, the Japanese love to play, and their gaiety is often riotous. Competitive games, games of chance, games of pretence or of solitaire are plentiful, but most of all the Japanese love the indoor games which bring them close to their cultural roots. The Heian period, suffused with the mysteries of its refinement, remains the perfect standard by which to define the Japanese soul. "Gazing at the moon" in autumn, "contemplating the flowers" in spring, "listening to the six-legged musicians" in summer, the deep emotion aroused by the thud of snow falling from a roof in winter – these are all experiences nostalgically shared with friends. The poetic mood evoked at these times is rediscovered in the indoor games which were prevalent at the Heian court. The fan was tossed during singing, poetry was written while drinking sake and shells were matched while listening to music. This game with shells was the basis for card games of the time. The two halves of the shells were painted with the same motif or poem. One half of each shell was placed on the floor and pairs had to be matched. The game of "one hundred poems by one hundred poets" was similar – the first part of a famous text was placed on the floor and the other half had to be found by drawing a text out at random. This game is still played at New Year.

Much less literary, but more popular, was the game of "flower cards" introduced into Japan by the Dutch at the beginning of the Edo period. It consists of twelve sets of four cards illustrated with flowers and trees which correspond to the twelve months of the year. Each series of cards has a value system according to whether it has a text or the picture of a symbolic object in addition to its floral illustration. There are several ways of playing with these cards. The most harmless version is adapted for children, while the most passionate and dangerous is only played by the *yakuza*, Japanese gangsters.

Many of these indoor games were no longer played after the military powers took over at the end of the

Paper balloon

Right and opposite:
Ane-sama from Shizuoka

Masu Suzuki only uses paper printed by stencil which comes from the regions of Tokyo and Echizen. She does however make an exception for ribbons of dyed cloth to attach the headdress. The faceless doll is designed to be presented in back view.

Dolls from Yamagata

Paper dolls from the Yamagata prefecture. Their originality stems from the treatment of their face in contrast with the simplicity of their body.

Contemporary doll

The exaggerated poses and luxurious paper are characteristic of recent experimentation in the field of the paper doll.

Geisha girls playing cards

Coloured photograph from the 1920s.

"Cards of one hundred poems"

12th century, as a more physical form of expression was then preferred, but these games came back into fashion at the end of the 15th century in castles and were especially popular during the Edo period. Using paper, craftsmen created new games for children's amusement: paper construction games, games with nests of boxes, paper balls or mills with sails made of *washi* and decorated with coloured motifs. All these novelties demonstrate that children the world over are fascinated by the same things.

Hana-karuta
"flower cards"

Paper in Art

In comparison with Western art, which loves certainties, Japanese art is never defined in a fixed and immutable form. The eternal quality of the masterpiece, the taste for the ruined building bequeathed by Greek civilisation and the dogmatic principles and references confirmed by Roman culture have no currency in Japan. Japanese artistic treatises are not the expression of aesthetic theory. More simply, they consist of knowledge passed down from generation to generation by respected masters. They perpetuate the teaching of the ancients to perfection, so that one day they can be equalled or exceeded. Creators who consider themselves to be artists are rare - most lay claim to being craftsmen instead, and this state of mind is apparent in what they produce. The Japanese artistic media all involve movement in space and rhythm in time. Painting develops dynamically, the *kimono* exists only to be worn, lacquers are always utilitarian and metal cannot be dissociated from the process which gives it form. All adapt and are renewed with the seasons, so that no painting ever adorns a wall permanently. Apart from in temples, no sculpture imposes its fixed shape upon a place of habitation. Even architecture contrives to be polyvalent and totally open to nature.

Paper reigns supreme in this subtle game of transformation. Architectural structure is defined by partitions, windows and screens, while rolls of paper, examples of calligraphy and lacquered paper objects enliven nooks and crannies. Even the occupants use paper to dress elegantly or create the artistic marvel of

Opposite:
Shoji

The graphic effect of shoji *frames.*

179

Shoji

The Nijo palace at Kyoto.

the *kimono*. Modernity has not weakened this fervour. Former aesthetic values and their rituals have recently been rediscovered, and the spirit of "paper" has also inspired much current research. Traditional *washi* is no longer necessarily the ideal vehicle for today's creations, but modern paper is also becoming established as a living, "user-friendly" and creative medium, whose qualities are no longer restricted to the context of the Japanese archipelago.

Paper in architecture

The Japanese house could not exist without paper. It is just as much an architectural material as wood or straw. All these materials are natural, so they interact with the elements - with humidity and dryness, shadow and sun, fire or snow. The Japanese are telling the truth when they say that their house breathes and trembles with them. The humanity of their environment is largely conditioned by the nature of paper. They love its whiteness which is never vulgar and is such a contrast to the coldness of marble or metal. They search for its natural imperfection, which communicates with them on an emotional level.

Shoji, the paper window

In a country of hot, humid summers and cold, bright winters, the ancient Japanese learned how to design a window capable of fulfilling both climatic and aesthetic needs. The *shoji* does not simply diffuse light, it also filters noise, tones down smells and transforms the air. Its presence lends the intimacy of the house a diffused atmosphere from which all aggression is excluded. Japanese dictums take on their true value in this context: "A noise is heard but not listened to", "the naked person can be seen but is not looked at". This cultural relationship between matter and man almost inevitably implies a poetic one. The play of shadows cast by trees, people and animals outside does not lend itself to reflection upon the relativity of things, but is understood instead as an expression of the refinement of nature and as an amusement for the spectator. When open, the *shoji* frames a piece of countryside which seems to invite itself into the house, since in Japan inside and outside are not separated by the barrier of a wall. The verandah of a traditional Japanese house, sheltered beneath a steeply sloping roof, forms part of the interior space, while at the same time being the threshold of the garden. A point of tension between the two, it sums up both. *Shoji* have an identical nature, whether they are fixed or sliding.

The Japanese window is a simple wooden lattice, mounted on a more solid frame. The outer surface is hung with *washi*, leaving the wooden frame visible from the inside. The paper is adapted to the dimen-

Shoji

The "tudy" corner of a traditional house.

181

Veranda *shoji*

sions of the frame - today standard sheets of paper measure 51x56cm, so four sheets are needed to cover a *shoji*. The strips are sold in rolls of about fifty sheets glued end to end. The paper used for *shoji* comes traditionally from Mino (Gifu), but by far the best is made in the village of Uchiyama, in the Nagano prefecture. It is only made during the winter and gets its perfect whiteness from being exposed to the snow.

Strong like all *washi*, *shoji* paper is not proof against tears. The replacement of damaged parts is a delicate operation, as the slightest difference in thickness, colour or material will cause the window to lose its visual unity. When damage is only slight, the Japanese stick on pieces of paper cut out and decorated with flo-

Shoji

It is necessary to kneel to open the sliding partitions.

**Screen from the
Edo period**

ral or geometric motifs, producing the most beautiful effect. This technique is reminiscent of those used on watermarked paper which was made from the 12th century onwards (and particularly from the 18th century onwards) to decorate the windows of the study corner in the main room. These marks, which were inserted in the sheet using waterproof paper shapes, often represented the householder's coat of arms or designs from nature such as waves.

In the middle of the 19th century, Western influence gradually introduced the glass window. It sometimes replaced the paper *shoji*, but usually duplicated it to provide better insulation. In both cases, there was a loss of light. The objects in the house no longer radiated soft reflected hues, the wood and *tatami* no longer trembled in the heat, and even shadow lost the mystery of its subtle gradations.

Tsuitate

Screen on feet in the Rin-so-in temple at Yaizu.

Paper partitions (*fusuma*) and screens (*byobu*)

In a house of very open design, facing outwards, the sheltered part offers total freedom of space. However, this space must be isolated from external aggressive influences such as noise, light or dust, and should afford privacy to its users. Paper windows partly fulfilled this requirement, but the demand for additional partitions arose at the end of the 7th century. At this time, a screen was offered to the Japanese court by Korean princes. Three centuries later, this piece of furniture was indispensable to all aristocratic homes. The first folding screens, called *byobu*, came from China, and consisted of four, six or twelve panels fastened together. Besides providing protection from draughts, these panels also became decorative items, with hinges made of paper. Painters and calligraphers tried their hand at this new creative medium. The intervention of art in furnishings became standard in the Heian period. Homes were then large open spaces with no fixed partitioning, the only real architectural separation being the one isolating the master's quarters from that of the rest of the family. The two parts of the building were linked by an outside corridor looking onto the garden to the south. It was not until the Muromachi period that living space was architecturally separated into areas with specific uses, such as a study and alcoves, and that a space was created which could be made into

separate units by sliding partitions and removable screens. Also at this time, and particularly during the Momoyama period, the decoration extended over the entire surface of a screen, and gold leaf was lavishly used to enhance the painted subject. Previously, each panel's decoration had been limited by the frame around each sheet of paper.

One form of screen still widely used is reminiscent of the first attempt to provide privacy and protection from draughts. This is the *tsuitate*, which is a single panel edged with wood, hung with decorated paper and mounted on feet. Originally very wide, it had the same function as the future sliding partitions.

The *fusuma* partition is manufactured in exactly the same way as the screen. It has a wooden lattice upon which paper is mounted. In general, six layers of paper are necessary for a good result. The work is tricky because of the tension between the sheets of paper and the wood, and is made even more difficult by the tension between the sheets of paper themselves. For this reason, not all the sheets are entirely covered in glue, and not all are the same size. Careful preparation is vital before applying the final sheet of paper which takes the painted decoration. In the past, craftsmen took care to make the surface uniform by covering it with thin sheets of very old paper such as pages from old books.

The word *fusuma* means "sleeping space" and is derived from the first use for these partitions: to partition off resting and sleeping space, a privileged area with décor appropriate to its tranquil, contemplative purpose. As in the case of the screens, poets and painters were called upon to illustrate them. In the Heian period, paper imported from China and Korea was used, and was called *kara-kami*, or "Chinese paper". This term was then used to refer to the printing technique used for all *fusuma* which were not painted directly by an artist, and especially that of scattering circular or oval prints all over the surface with a small, carved wooden block. In the 12th century, the decoration was perfected by gluing on at regular intervals small sheets which had been block-printed separately. This was the beginning of the crafting of Japanese "Chinese paper", which underwent a spectacular development during the Muromachi and Momoyama periods, in direct competition with Indian ink painting done by Zen Buddhist followers. Once again, the Edo period made Japanese craftsmanship available to the townspeople, who could all equip their houses with "painted paper" printed using the *karakami* technique. For almost three centuries, this technique was to improve and to cause the rapid development of designs printed on the twelve sheets of paper which were required to decorate one side of a partition. The Meiji period brought about a striking innovation with an increase in the size of the carved wooden blocks, which meant that ten sheets could be printed and glued to each other on the panel. Soon, the printing operation was to be reduced even further with the invention of a double block with a symmetrically repeated motif. Now it was sufficient to bring the paper into contact with the block five times, and this considerably reduced the time taken to make the decoration.

The paper used often comes from the Hyogo region, which formerly produced a paper coated with clay containing gold or silver. The printing technique is curious. The carved wooden block is inked using a frame resembling the former Korean *uchiwa*, which is covered with cotton previously smeared with colour. The sheet of paper is then placed on the wood and rubbed to reveal the design. Usually this operation is done twice to ensure that the colour has taken well. Locating the patterns precisely and, above all, achieving unity of colour on each decorated sheet remain the most difficult parts of the process.

The colour quality is as astonishing as the method of printing. The colour itself is composed of pigment and a glue extracted from an alga known as "pretty seaweed" because of its unusual texture. A small amount of rice powder is added to speed up drying, as is shell or mica powder to create a subtle effect under light. The motifs are designed to be easy on the eye and not to attack the senses, especially in the case of large scale decorations. When an entire wall is composed of *fusuma* made from "Chinese paper", it is important not to emphasise the repetition of the motif. Mica or shell powder is used since motifs may not be entirely visible in the light filtered by the *shoji*. The effect is even more subtle in lantern light.

Other techniques have been used by *karakami* craftsmen such as lacquering, applying multiple colours, superimposing two dyes and creasing the paper to obtain a moiré background, and setting off colours with gold, silver or mica sequins. The range of

Production

Top:
Applying colour to the printing block.
Bottom:
Binding agent for the colour and "pretty seaweed" for making glue.

Opposite, top:
Sticking the paper onto a mini sliding door.
Bottom:
Craftsman's tools for making partitions.

Karakami

Above:
*Wooden printing block
for the paper used to
make partitions.*

Left and right:
Sheets of finished
karakami.

Karakami

*Materials for printing
luxury* karakami: *gold
leaf and powder, silver
powder, lacquer
spatula and pads.*

Karakami

*Partition decorated
with* karakami.

motifs is extremely varied. Kenichi Senda, whose family has practised this skill for eleven generations, owns 600 carved wooden printing blocks. The oldest dates from 1792 - it is practically impossible to find examples older than this because of the civil wars that took place at the end of the 18th century. A perfectionist, he refuses to collect wood blocks made after 1926, which he believes is when *karakami* went into its final deline. Today, Kenichi Senda is one of the rare craftsmen who use this technique in all its former purity. For this reason he was given the task of renewing the partitions of the Katsura imperial villa in Kyoto. Most of the motifs preserved in his collection represent so-called "palace" décors: stylised waves, cartwheels decorated with flowers, the more abstract rhythms of broken stripes or mediaeval squared surfaces, plant seedlings, herbs and animals which were favourites in the Edo period. In contrast, the wood blocks from the Meiji period show the growing influence of subjects inspired by the West and a loss of national taste.

Like many craftsmen, he believes that a minimum apprenticeship is necessary to practise his art. The liking for hierarchic rituals between master and apprentices and a love of the symbolic system of numbers means that five years' work is required to achieve ideal proportions between the pictorial constituents, the paper quality and the delicacy of the wood block. Ten years are required to perfect the unity of printing itself, and it takes fifteen years to learn how to lift a perfectly printed sheet of paper off an old block which has been warped by time and human misfortune.

The art of *karakami* lives again today as more of an art than a craft, although such a differentiation has never truly existed in Japan. As in the beginning, it is reserved for a cultural élite which refuses to abandon the values of traditional Japanese feeling. Fortunately, the new creators - architects, decorators, stylists and designers - have made a quality environment a necessity by restoring the taste for noble materials and unadulterated techniques. The paper used for *shoji* and *fusuma* still remains the ideal reference when conjuring up an image of the Japanese house.

In spite of its modernity, the Japanese house is still often placed under the sign of paper and of the ancestral gods. Skilled carpenters would not know how to build it without consecrating it as they did in the past. When a new framework has been assembled, the *tate-*

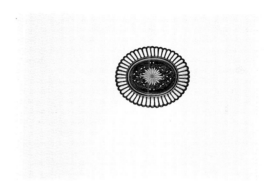

Karakami

Detail from opposite page.

mae ceremony takes place during which strips of paper are attached to the ridgepole to obtain protection from the gods. If the building is large, the ceremony is on a grander scale and may take place at a large shrine where the ridgepole is completely covered in virgin paper and presented to the *kami*.

Paper for art

Paintings, prints and calligraphy

If not all civilisations have developed a paper art as inventive as that of Japan, all have used paper as a medium for their memory. The documentary evidence of historians, the written reports of state servants, the written prayers of monks or the written expression of feelings by poets and novelists are the most obvious examples. Writing is not at all confined to the transcription of words - its mastery is immediately accompanied by majesty to magnify ideas. Calligraphy has thus become a dialogue with paper, which Eastern and Far Eastern letters have learned to exploit to the very limits of legibility. There is a fine line between calligraphy and painting. With organised colour, the memory of men becomes the memory of the world. The whole universe is expressed on paper to transcribe what words alone simply cannot state - the essence of man.

In 610, the Korean painter Dam Ching showed the Japanese court how to make ink with a stick of soot and how to draw the first ideograms of Japanese history. His art was the pinnacle of skill, as the paintbrush had existed in China for nearly 1000 years. He laid the foundations for the standardisation of writing media, and thus, after much trial and error, for the birth of paper. Painting developed in the Nara period under Buddhist guidance without being in a position to rival statuary. Calligraphy, however, had its moments of glory.

The Heian period brought the two modes together in a typically Japanese form of expression, where the rhythms of one interweave closely with the lines of the other. Through the impetus of esoteric sects, painting became laden with symbols and stole the lead over sculpture. Calligraphy competed with it to define the golden rules which would remain current until the 19th century. This process of creating art in the Japanese

Opposite:
Calligraphy

Calligraphy by Mrs Yasue.

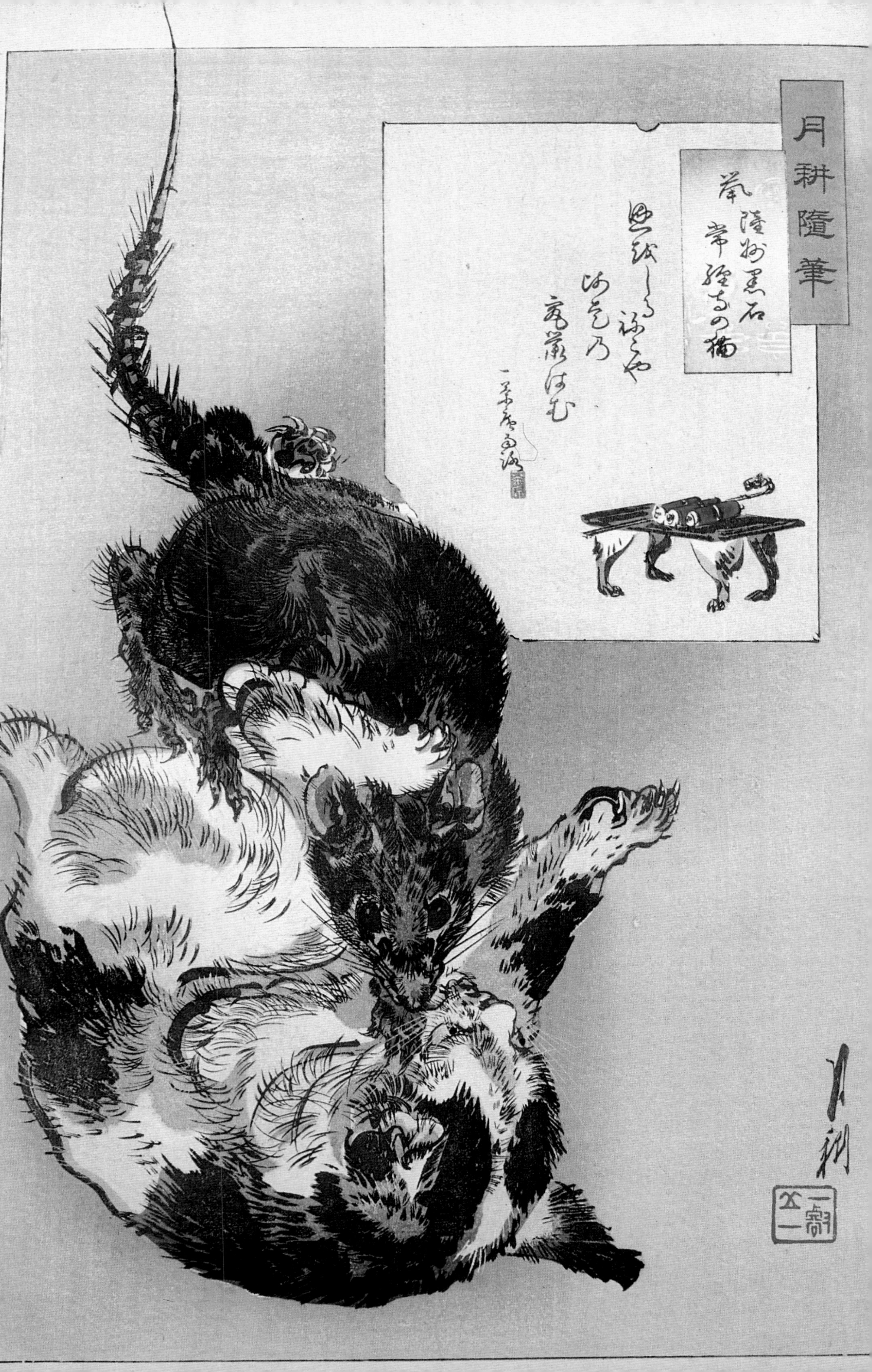
月耕隨筆

style took effect at a time when the world of aristocrats eclipsed that of the monks. It was then as relevant in women's quarters as in the offices of state and religious officials. The invention of *kana* syllabaries (8th and 9th centuries), which were easier to draw than Chinese ideograms, gave rise to the birth of a court literature which was more poetic than religious, and which found concrete expression in the 10th century in the exceptional novel written by a woman called Murasaki Shikibu, the *Story of Genji*. These syllabaries perfectly complemented drawing, particularly of landscapes, and genre painting, both of which were then emerging. "Japanese painting" thus predominated over "Chinese painting" and painters achieved real status in society.

Screen

Screen *made of two sheets of paper decorated with calligraphy.*

Opposite:
Print by Ogata Gekko (1859-1920).

Chirigi-e

*Torn paper painting
by Setsuko Masuda.*

The Kamakura period was more realist and intellectual than the Heian period. Landscape backgrounds appeared frequently on painted rolls. These also became longer and longer, to allow the many adventures related in fashionable novels to be used as subject matter for designs. The portrait also became a major art form, with high Buddhist and court dignitaries being painted. Adventurous monks brought back new systems of belief from China, and with them the styles of art and calligraphy in vogue on the continent. Among these, Zen Buddhism was to leave an indelible mark upon Japanese culture. Calligraphy was becoming more widespread, but sometimes also more abstruse, often ending up as totally illegible, the sign of an intellectual pursuit dominated by aesthetics. In the 15th century, the master Sesshu immortalised painting using an Indian ink wash, a model production of Zen perfection. During this fertile century, the first lines of professional painters such as the Kanos became established. Their creations were a successful compromise between powerful coloured decorative painting, the "Chinese" pictorial strokes of Zen, and "Japanese painting", always valued by the aristocracy. This style developed naturally during the Momoyama period, a time when many castles and residences were built. Sliding partitions and screens were decorated with rich colours and gold leaf. Everything was bigger and more magnificent than before. Even the subjects of painting changed to include people, and genre paintings multiplied as did the stories about strange visitors to the archipelago at the end of the century. Famous Japanese prints showed these "Southern barbarians" with blond or red hair, excessively long noses and strange customs.

The Edo civilisation only confirmed these tendencies. Popular culture turned towards an extreme liveliness of expression in the face of official trends, which were

still dependent upon pictorial and calligraphic conventions dating from the preceding decades. The Kano, Soga and Tosa schools produced classical designs, but artists like Sotatsu and Korin reacted against this dogmatism by reviving the aristocratic elegance of the Heian period, enhanced with a new freedom and vigour. There was great enthusiasm among ordinary people for prints, whose creation allowed pictures to be distributed widely. Woodcuts were not new, as examples exist dating back to 764, but they were limited to the printing of Buddhist texts and to the dyeing of certain fabrics. It was not until the 17th century or thereabouts that printing was transformed into a real means of communication. In the 1650s, Moronobu Hishikawa used wood engraving for far less noble subjects. The eventful lives of courtesans and *kabuki* actors became the basis for what were called "images of the floating world" (*ukiyo-e*) in 1682. Depicting the worlds of the ephemeral, of pleasure and of fashion, the Moronobu print is an example of a truly popular form of expression, which was constantly enriched in colour and subtlety. The beauties of the Edo period and their fervent admirers, the affected play-actors and their colourful spectators, as well as the intimate scenes of young people's education were soon complemented by observations of city life in all its variety. Fashionable novels were illustrated, the passion for travel was a pretext for painting Mount Fuji in all its moods, news was first reported in this way... until the West found in this a lively source of European artistic renewal at the end of the 19th century.

The first examples of printing appeared in the form of single pages or books with black or red print, sometimes embellished with a single colour. Towards 1720, a more varied chromatic range was used, ending up with a dozen different shades laid on by successive printing. A painter, an engraver and a printer were required to produce them. The artist worked freely on very thin paper which served as an engraving guide for the sculpting craftsman. The printer then used all his art - in particular his knowledge of papers and their nine standard formats - to make the print. Echizen paper, made at Fukui, is generally considered to be the best suited to prints, but the choice of medium depends on the subject and its size. Special papers like *torinoko* were often used for their plastic quality. The latter is the colour of "eggshell", which combines very well with a faint design. Many artists coated their papers with a mixture of glue and alum to prevent the paper becoming too dirty while it was being work on, but this was not essential. When prepared in this way, the paper had to be moistened one hour before printing. Echizen paper, and particularly the variety called *hosho*, is ideal for prints, as it is for calligraphy. It is thick, strong, downy, creamy white and absorbent. This last quality is essential when working with Indian ink which responds to the rhythm of the writing, revealing the tensions,

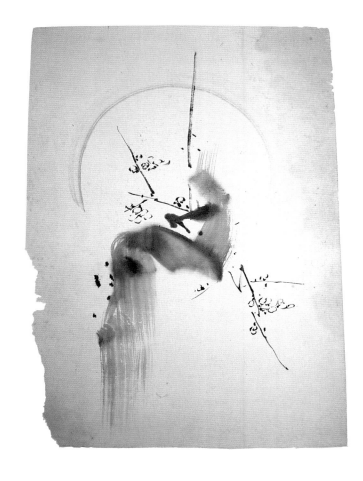

Craftsman's study

Elegant draft design on paper for the decoration of porcelain. The sheets of paper, subsequently perforated and dabbed with soot, reproduced the motif of the object.

Geisha's visiting cards

Printed on chiyogami, *these cards changed every half season.*

acceleration, soaring movements, strong lines and even the "silences" present in the calligraphic act. It was greatly loved by noblemen and noblewomen of the Muromachi period for writing on, before its range of uses was extended to include ceremonial wrapping. It was not the only type of paper - others favoured by the Heian court have retained their specific character down the ages, in particular *gasen-shi*, which is made from *mitsumata* mixed with fibres of bamboo, straw, cotton and recycled paper.

Whereas the standard print used nine different formats, calligraphy used four. In the Heian period, *kaishi* (literally "pocket paper") was slipped into the *kimono* sleeve of nobles who were still disposed to write poetry. It was a sheet of thick paper, either white or coloured, and was almost square in format. The characters of thirty-one syllable poems, derived from the Chinese, were written on it, and it was often mounted on a vertical roll. It was also used in the tea ceremony, not as a writing medium, but rather for cleaning the part of the bowl touched by the lips. *Shikishi* also had an almost square format, but was smaller. It was also used for painting, and was frequently stuck onto cardboard and hung on the wall. *Tanzaku* had an elongated rectangular format. It could be white or decorated, and was used for thirty-one syllable poems, or for *haiku*, which had seventeen syllables. Lastly, the *semmen* was a cutout in the shape of a fan, which came in different sizes, and was used as much for painting as for writing poetry.

Paper was also used on its own in the composition of "paintings". This technique of collage using torn paper was called *chigiri-e*. The process is an old one, as it was used in the Heian period to make certain papers for poetry writing. More recently, this technique was used to create real paper paintings. The material has to be thin and very fibrous to allow superimposed colours to mix together through the interaction of the papers and the effects of transparency. The artist attaches great importance to the quality of the dyes used on the paper. The rest is a matter of taste, as the slightest false move reduces the result to a simple example of manual work, devoid of all artistic power.

Another means of expression deserves to be mentioned within the body of Japanese artistic production, namely the embossed paper the Japanese call "leather paper". It was first made in the Edo period to replace

Chiyogami

Decorative paper printed by stencil.

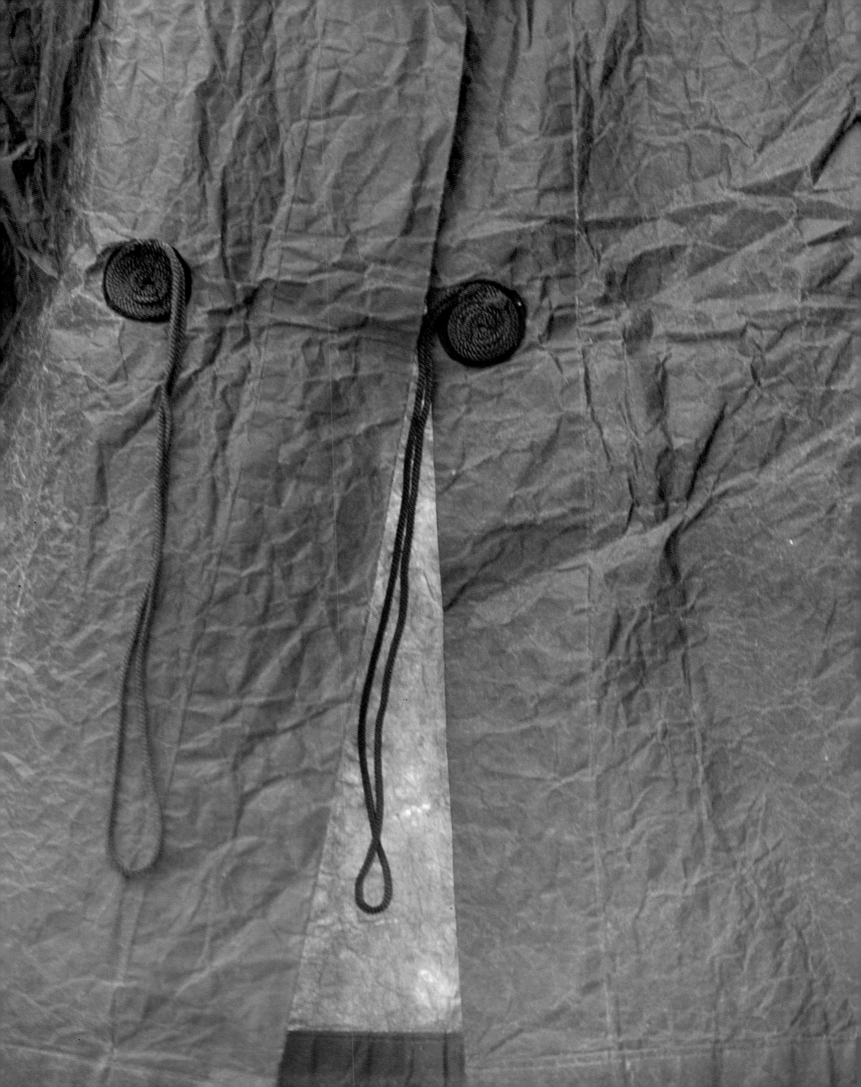

the tooled leather used, for example, in the making of armoured breastplates. Buddhism got the better of this craft, and the production of effective arms could no longer be justified in peacetime. So imitation leather was made by pressing soaked paper on cloth or straw matting to produce a slightly embossed effect. It was then oiled and lacquered. In the 19th century, when the shapes for printing in relief were engraved on cylinders made of cherry wood, the embossing of paper became a truly artistic technique. The repertoire subsequently expanded to include designs in the shape of arabesques, interlacing patterns, bird and plant motifs. Everyday objects, such as boxes, purses and snuffboxes, were adorned with this delicate lacquered relief.

Paper and the *kimono*

The *kimono* is one of the artistic media most characteristic of Japan. Whether it is made of fibres of nettle, hemp, flax, cotton or silk, its surface is a single unit, which will fit any size or shape of person. The strips from which it is made have no darts or pleats for shaping it to the anatomy. Two triangular bands alone position it around the neck and chest. The roll of material from which the garment is made is an ideal medium for artistic expression, from simple indigo dyeing to the marvels of brocade and embroidery. Some of these techniques used paper as a tool or as a basis for the creation itself. The technique of drawing directly onto silk, as practised by *yuzen* craftsmen, cannot be performed without a cone of waterproof paper which is used to draw the lines of glue before the colour is applied. In the weaving of brocades, cards of perforated paper have been used since the importation of Jacquard and Battan looms in the 19th century. In tie-dyeing, the areas to be kept free of dye are protected with waterproof paper, which is tied onto the designs. In all these cases, the paper is a tool which could easily be replaced with other materials. In the art of stencil printing, however, it is irreplaceable.

Kata-gami, the stencil, came to Japan from Korea. In the 9th century an important production centre had already been established at Ise, not far from the great shrine dedicated to the Sun Goddess, which seems to indicate that it was used for religious purposes. In the Kamakura period, stencil printing became more wides-

Kamiko

The three stages of kamiko *paper production: right to left, creasing, waterproofing and oiling.*

pread and was used for the clothes of warriors, who preferred more sober attire than the Kyoto aristocrats. After the *shogun* were again tempted by the splendour of the imperial capital, the stencil technique fell into decline for nearly three centuries until the Edo period, when it was taken up again and adapted for printing silk.

There are many local varieties of stencil printing. The designs and colour ranges differ, but the principle remains the same. The *kata-gami* is the masterpiece of the technique. Only *kozo* or *mitsumata* paper is suitable, usually that produced in Gifu or Hiroshima. The stencil is meticulously cut using scissors from a card made up of three or four sheets of paper, stuck together with the tannin from the persimmon plant, in a standard 36x76cm format (sometimes 36x91cm). Each stencil is extremely strong, as it has to be used several times and must be totally resistant to glue, colorants and the rinsing water, which always follows each application of colour. To comply with these requirements, the paper has to undergo special treatment. It is brushed with persimmon juice, placed to dry on a plank in the sun, then smoked for twelve days before being daubed with persimmon again. To make the cutout shapes, it is wise to use paper which is two or three years old, particularly when the designs are delicate or very close together as in the printing of small motifs called *komon* ("little coats of arms"). The four-centuries-old *komon* was originally intended for printing coats of arms on ceremonial *kimonos*. It was then reduced to a scattering of small varied designs for covering the entire surface of ordinary people's clothing. However, when the decoration is much larger or the cutout too delicate, silk gauze is inserted between the sheets of paper to hold the cutout shapes or sometimes to block them out completely. This type of collage takes many long years of practice, for it is crucial that there should be no gap between the two superimposed parts of the stencil.

The stencil, cut away in accordance with the drawing and marked with positional guides, is placed on the roll of previously glued fabric on the workbench. Using a wooden spatula, extra glue is spread over the cutout, leaving the shape of the drawing in negative form. The rest of the fabric is then dyed using a brush, before being heated and washed to eliminate any traces of rice glue. The two-coloured design can then be seen,

Weaving

Weaving paper and cotton to make peasant clothing.

Production

Top left:
A cone of waterproof paper, used to apply glue when employing the yuzen *technique.*
Top right and bottom left and right:
Direct printing using a brush.

with its outlines as crisp as if it were printed. In the more refined technique known as *kata-yuzen*, the stencil is used not to print in negative form, but to dye the motif positively, the cutout corresponding directly to each colour planned. This means that there are as many stencils as there are colours in the design. The most magnificent have up to fifty colours, and it takes five or six months to make the stencils. The craftsman puts the stencils on one by one, corresponding to the colours and always starting with the stencil for black writing or patterning. Depending on the accuracy of the motifs, he uses the wooden spatula, a round brush or even a small retouching brush to put the finishing touches to the gradations.

Stencil

The art of the stencil became a necessity during the Second World War. In the absence of cloth, the Japanese were often obliged to dress in kamiko *decorated with stencils.*

The repeated applications of dye based on rice glue give Japanese colours their unmatched transparency and luminosity, qualities claimed by many regional traditions. The best known example is the incomparable *bingata* dye, used for generations by the sovereigns of the islands of Ryu-Kyu and Okinawa. *Bingata* is ideal for printing *kimonos* made from cotton or banana fibre: and its current vogue is due to the widespread movement for the restoration of popular arts, and in particular to the key figure of Keisuke Serizawa, who has devoted himself to the promotion of this southern technique of "dyeing with vivid colours".

Where clothing is concerned, paper is not merely an auxiliary to textiles: it can also be the only material used. *Kamiko*, the paper garment, was used from the 11th century onwards to make undergarments for the monks of esoteric sects. The monks of the Nigatsu-do temple at Nara still wear a paper *kimono* for the O-mizu-tori festival. As in the past, women still do not have the right to touch this consecrated *kimono*, which must remain absolutely unblemished when the officiating priests lay a camellia flower on the statue of the Buddha. In the Edo period, the *kamiko* lost its specifically religious connotations and was worn by the ordinary people. It was no longer used solely as a warm undergarment, but was also worn as a jacket, belt or even as a scarf. Samurai, poets, tea masters and artists adopted it for its aesthetic simplicity. The nobility edged it with silk at the collar and sleeves, or used it as a lining for their silk *kimono*. Some liked it dyed simply with persimmon juice, others preferred it to be dazzling white. In all cases, it was worn creased, as it became soft and manageable directly on contact with body heat. As for the poor, they had nothing else to wear. Their makeshift mattresses were also made of the same material, and this had the great advantage of repelling vermin, which had to make do with straw and cloth mattresses instead.

The technique of making *kamiko* is extremely simple. Kozo paper, now mainly from Kyoto and Sendai, is creased by hand before being coated in persimmon juice or *konnyaku* (arum root mucilage). *Konnyaku* is used when the paper must stay white or when it is to receive a painted design. The sheets of paper are glued end to end to make a roll of standard length as for *kimonos* made of fabric, before being cut and assembled in strips. When the garment has to be waterproofed against rain, it is also dipped in flax or sesame oil.

The only difficulty with *kamiko* lies in the production of its paper, whose fibres must run at right angles to each other, so that the finished product is resistant to tearing in all directions.

Another category of clothing derives its uniqueness from paper. *Kamiko* is designed for winter, but *shifu* is essentially for the summer. It is a "cloth" made of threads of paper, invented around 1650 for the pleasure of the ruling class. Formerly it was no more than a crude weave of wide strips of recycled paper which peasants wore in areas where *washi* was produced. From the Edo period onwards, it became a speciality in the Sendai region thanks to the overlord of Shiroishi, who considerably assisted its development. The *shifu* of this clan was particularly fine in texture, and thus became a luxury object arousing great enthusiasm among the overlords of that time. *Kozo* fibres were worked as they floated, so they could be arranged in lines to make the paper easier to cut. A clever design of parallel cutouts then allowed a single continuous ribbon to be drawn from the sheet, which only had to be rolled over on itself to produce a thread. A ball of thread one hundred metres long could then be made up, which served to weave not only the outdoor jackets that were worn over the *kimono*, *samurai* clothes but also the "shoulder garment" which these warriors wore over their *kimono*-trouser outfit. It was also used for cushions, mosquito nets, and for "reading" suits which were put on at night. Depending on the quality required, the weft was woven in paper and the warp in cotton or silk, or else the whole frame was woven in paper. A special feature of this exceptional material was that it could be washed like cloth.

These paper threads could also be lacquered. This was done when they were used for lacing up parade armour in the Edo period, and for making bags, hats, water and powder flasks, boxes and baskets. Even sandals were braided using this process, the results being much more robust than ordinary sandals made of straw.

Paper which had been lacquered over its entire surface was also an adjunct to Japanese costume. It could be used to make clothes chests, like those still used by *sumo* wrestlers, or as the basic material of certain clothing accessories such as hats.

Above and opposite:
Kimono chests

Making kimono *chests for* sumo *wrestlers. These chests are made of paper stuck to a bamboo framework. The whole item is then lacquered and embossed with the coat of arms of the wrestler.*

Below:
Chiyogami

Chiyogami *today is often printed on certain popular consumer objects such as this child's box.*

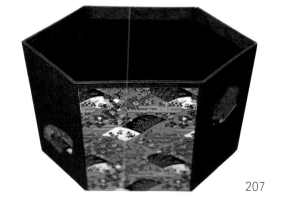

Headaddresses

*From left to right:
Headdresses of lacque-
red paper worn by*
bunkaru *puppets.
Opposite, below left:
Headdress of lacquered
paper worn during a*
shinto *ceremony.*

Headdresses were a very important element in the costume of ancient Japan. Under Chinese influence they had become a visual means of distinguishing the degrees of nobility of courtesans and the rank of state officials. The ribbons attaching them were dyed in different colours to accentuate this hierarchy. Later, with the advent of the military regime, the headdress became an aid to identification, as each clan had its own particular shape. It was then the custom to offer it up amid great ceremony when the sons of warriors came of age. This *eboshi* was originally made of cloth, but it was soon made of waterproofed and lacquered paper, shaped according to the form it took when flattened by the wind or by a warrior's helmet. Up until the Edo period, it was worn only by warriors, so when peace came it gradually disappeared, except in dance and *shinto* religion. Today it is still part of the official costume of priests.

The *jingasa* is another form of military headdress in lacquered paper. It was originally a flat metal helmet for servants at arms who followed knights into battle. With the introduction of arquebuses at the end of the 16th century, these "nimble legs", transformed into an army of infantrymen, wore *jingasa* embossed with the family arms of the commander of each company. As there were large numbers of these infantrymen, their head-

"Cake ship"

"Cake ship" by
Toshimichi Hiroi, 1985.

gear was made of lacquered paper instead of metal. At that time it was a simple flattened cone, but during the Edo period it took on increasingly elaborate shapes and was adopted by the lords on parade at the *shogun's* court, who decorated it with painted motifs or gold leaf.

Japanese soldiers used lacquered paper for many other items of their equipment. The baton of command was none other than a whip made of red and white or gold and silver lacquered paper. Clan standards were made of oiled paper and, from the end of the 16th century onwards, their poles were enhanced with symbolic papier-mâché sculptures. At this time, infantrymen equipped with arquebuses carried various lacquered paper boxes containing grapeshot cartridges (with canisters made of waterproof paper), boxes of wicks, and a storage case for the gun itself. As civilians were to do later, they wore waterproof clothing made of oiled paper on rainy days - a fashion imported from Portugal, whilst the rear-guard protected their equipment with large covering sheets made of the same material. From the end of the clan wars, archers' quivers were no longer made of braided reeds, but from threads of lacquered paper. Finally, it is worth noting that paper played a part during the Second World War. The Japanese command had planned to send bomb balloons over the United States. These balloons measured up to ten metres in diameter and were filled with hydrogen. They were made of waterproofed sheets of *kozo* glued together with *konnyaku*. Some of them reached their target.

Fun wrapping

Fun wrapping by Katsu Kimura.

Contemporary creations

In the West, the word "paper" in the context of art meant a medium for drawing and painting. This was the case until the two-dimensional space of painting was shattered by the Cubists, Dadaists and Surrealists. With the invention of collage, paper was promoted to the status of artistic tool, and even its poorest expression, the newspaper, revealed this inescapable tendency. Its qualities and defects became the accomplices of the artist and the translator of his creation. Inclusion, cutting, tearing, repairing, creasing and all the other treatments inflicted on this material became the basis for a new artistic vocabulary. Thus the West rediscovered techniques which Japan had itself discovered centuries ago in the art of daily life.

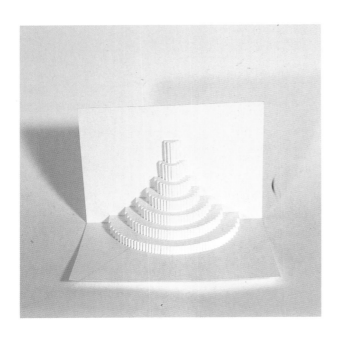

"Origamic architecture"

Study by Masahiro Chatani. A professor of architecture, Chatani has produced card cut-outs for self-assembly, which represent the main classics of world architecture.

Japan itself needed to rediscover this language, neglected for decades to the benefit of a Western-biased cultural exoticism. *Washi* was consumed in the fire of modernity. It had no place in a race towards the future. Only art preserved it from oblivion.

The rediscovery of popular traditions was sanctioned by the first international conference of craftsmanship in Kyoto in 1978. This recalled the universality of ancestral knowledge and restored its vocabulary in the service of contemporary creation. Japanese artists were thus able to revisit the roots of their sensibility, even if some had renounced "Japanese paper" (*washi*) in favour of "Western paper" (*yo-shi*). The fact still remains that their work stems from the same love of the material, from the same demand for quality that the craftsmen of the past placed at the service of all. The idea of conceptual space extolled by Shoichi Ida was echoed in the creations of Ko Morishima and also by Kyoko Ibe's attempts to create architectural space in which *washi* and light interact. The lanterns of Isamu Noguchi have the same soul as the *kamiko* of Itsuko Ueda or Issey Miyake. The works made of *washi* and iron threads by Katsuo Kawaguchi or Yoshio Kitayama are emotionally linked to the paper mobiles of Maki Nakagawa, Kazumasa Nagai's embossed paper and Hideaki Tomooka's landscapes on paper. Finally, the sculptured cutouts in Western paper by Hiroshi Ogawa, Kisa Kawakami or Motozo Yoshizaki have no other equal than the "origamic architecture" of Masahiro Chatani, the piled up structures of Shigeo Shinjo, the "fantasy papers" of Toshimichi Hiroi or the cardboard cult objects of Katsuhiko Hibino, to mention only the important artists.

Artistic craftsmen today are scarcely distanced from artists who use paper. Their works, the fruit of long hours of effort, somtimes attain the same prizes as those of their "rivals". This appears to be due to an incredible change in mentality. Since the Second World War, the West has become the ideal reference for many Japanese people. European culture seems better than theirs because it is suffused with the fragrance of an art of living which has acquired the patina of time, and whose ancient traces are concrete elements and not merely poetic memories of the past. As Wakao Fujioka states in an article on *The secret of high class*: "If people attach sufficient value to an object to accept its purchase at a very high price, it is because it beauti-

"Park"

"Park" by Hideaki Tomooka, 1990. This artist plays with all the different facets of paper treatment: perforation, moulding, collage, folding, braiding etc.

Left:
"Love letter"

"Love letter" by Shigeo Shinjo, 1990-1991. From paper engraving to paper on its own, Shinjo works the concept of accumulation and superimposition of the paper and its shadow.

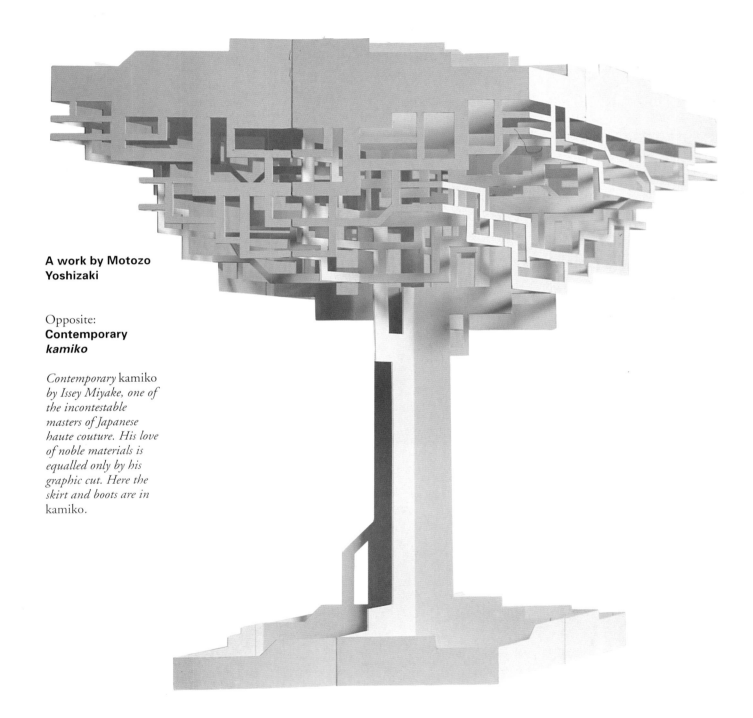

A work by Motozo Yoshizaki

Opposite:
Contemporary *kamiko*

Contemporary kamiko *by Issey Miyake, one of the incontestable masters of Japanese haute couture. His love of noble materials is equalled only by his graphic cut. Here the skirt and boots are in* kamiko.

fies the time which they intend to reserve for themselves'. His argument is mainly based on the purchase of the Western luxury article, but its logic may be applied to the craftsmanship of Japanese art. It should be stated that while many craftsmen continue to work within the ancient logical system of utilitarian objects, their children are increasingly orienting their technique towards the production of objects for exhibition. The admirers of these creations, which boast an extreme aesthetic refinement, are prepared to spend a fortune to acquire them. Designers make great use of them to define new spaces where the work of art can again become, as it once traditionally was, the centre of interest in the house. The current tendency for open space punctuated only by a number of significant creations has become the rule in the layout of fashionable shops, the quality of the materials alone defining the idea of *chic*, which has proven vital to the contemporary Japanese. Paper in all its forms is again part of the creators' display, and it is very likely that the power of its universal appeal will never be diminished.

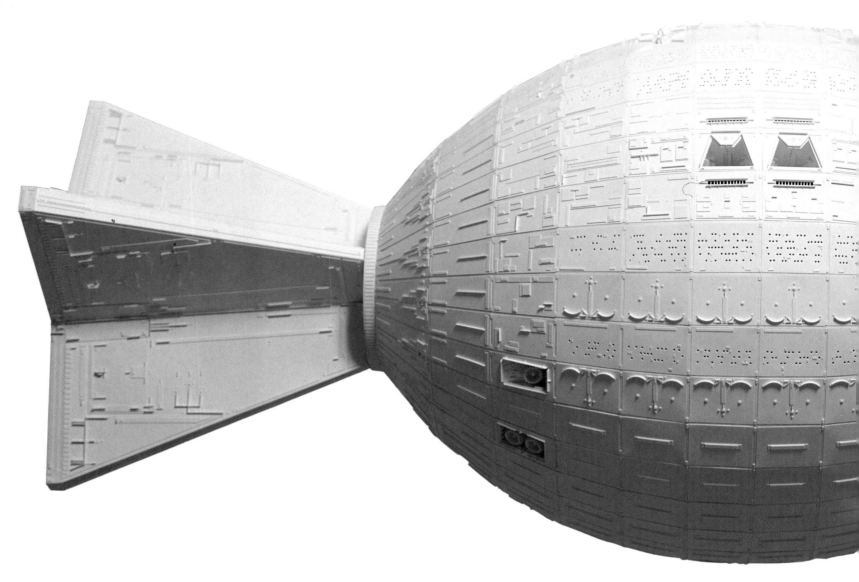

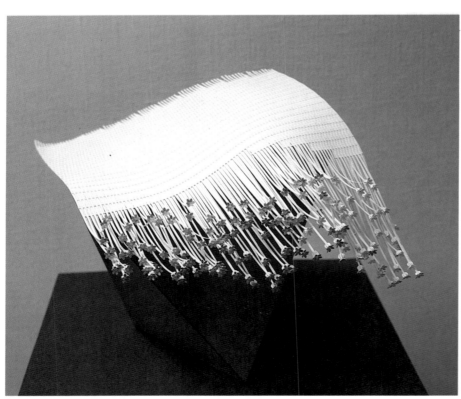

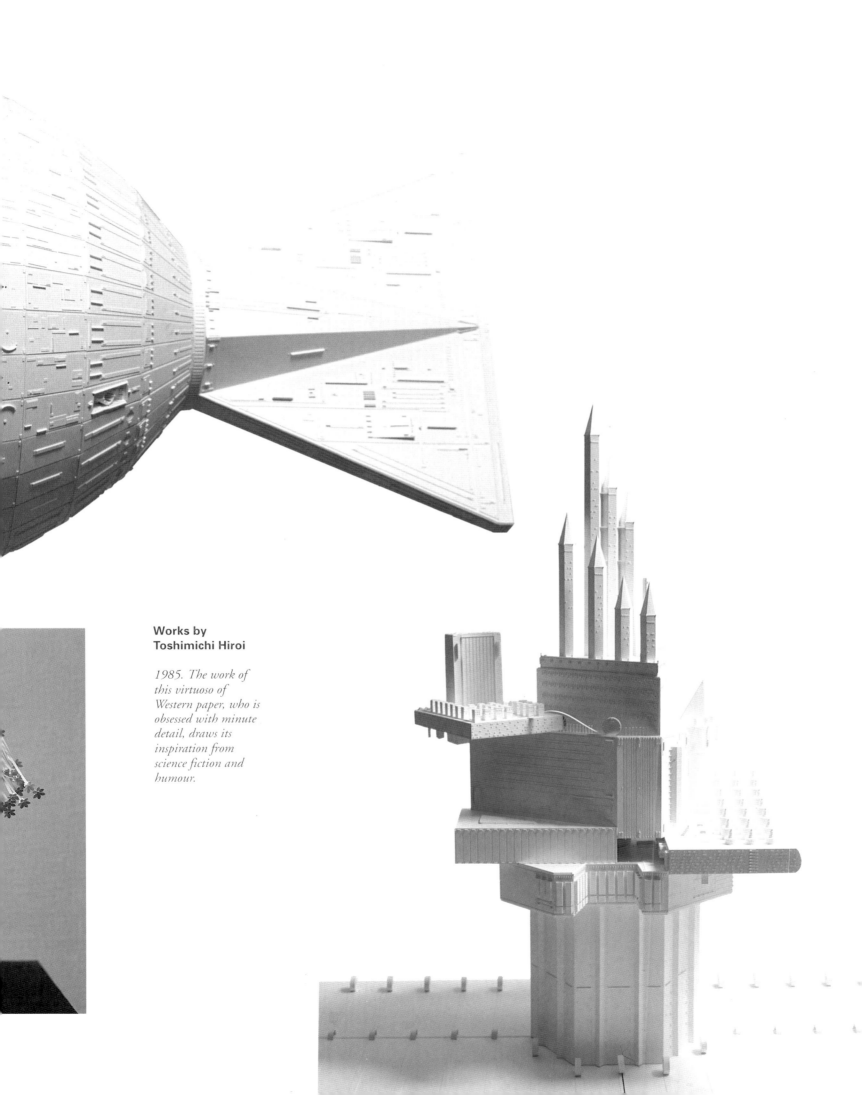

**Works by
Toshimichi Hiroi**

*1985. The work of
this virtuoso of
Western paper, who is
obsessed with minute
detail, draws its
inspiration from
science fiction and
humour.*

Origami study

*Study of modular
structures in* origami.
*Yoshihide Momotani is
one of the leaders in
this field.*

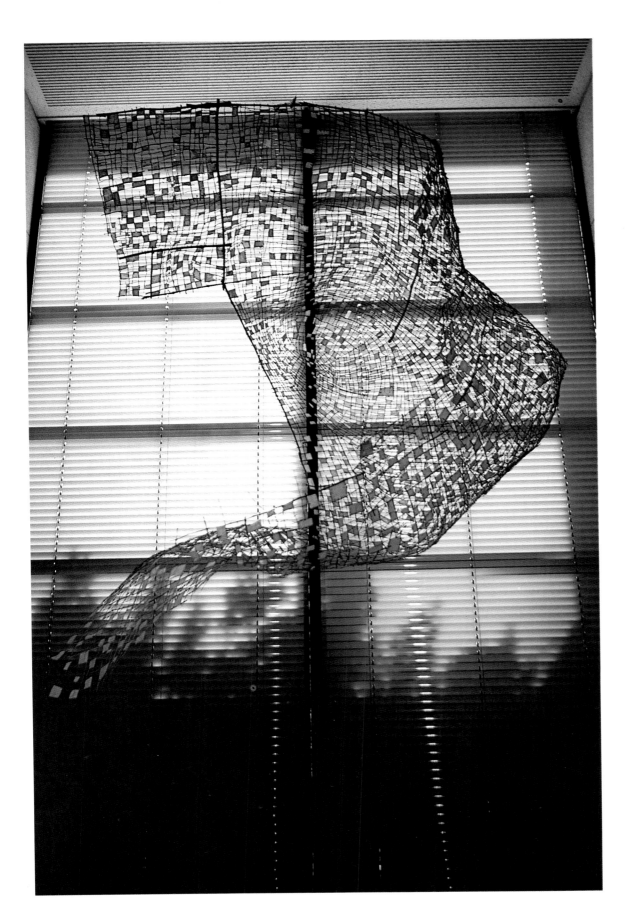

"Sake koko dewa"

Work of paper and iron threads by Yoshio Kitayama, 1987. Kitayama's work interacts in the spatial rhythm and tension between his structures and the environment. This work is in the Meguro Municipal Museum in Tokyo.

Overleaf:
"On the wind"

Mobile environment by Maki Nakagawa. The delicacy of this work, the sense of chromatic value and the subtle and moving play of the shadows created by it are reminiscent of the aristocratic and poetic art of the Heian imperial court. Its very contemporary construction has the same spirit of emotion, of the ephemeral and of illusion.

Glossary

ANE-SAMA (NINGYO): paper doll.

BAN-GASA: a parasol with simple decoration, so called because tradesmen would write a number on each one before lending them to customers.

BINGATA: a style of decoration stencilled on Okinawa kimonos.

BOMBORI: street lamp.

BON or O-BON: Festival of Souls.

BUNRAKU: puppet theatre.

BYOBU: folding screen.

CHIGIRI-E: artistic technique of painting with torn coloured paper.

CHOCHIN: folding lamp for outside use.

CHUKEI: ceremonial fan with the special feature of maintaining its flared shape even when closed.

DANSHI: a grade of paper, used by men in the Heian period to write poems in Chinese ideograms.

EBOSHI: originally worn by men in armour, this was a cap which folded beneath the helmet, before becoming a ceremonial headdress.

FUKI-ZOME: technique for dyeing paper by spraying.

FUSUMA: sliding partition covered in painted or printed paper.

GAMPI: *diplomorpha sikokiana*, a plant specific to Japan which is used in the manufacture of paper.

GEISHA: "woman skilled in the Arts"; originally a courtesan of the pleasure districts, today she is the living symbol of traditional arts of pleasing.

GIFU-JOCHIN: Gifu lantern.

GOFU: shinto amulet.

GOHEI: shinto offering consisting of paper cut out and folded in a zigzag.

GUNBAI: flat war fan.

HAIKU: seventeen syllable poem (5, 7, 5).

HARAI-GUSHI: shinto instrument of purification.

HARIKO: papier-mâché article.

HIKI-ZOME: technique of dyeing paper using a brush.

HINA-MATSURI: Festival of Dolls or Festival of Girls on 3rd March.

HOSHO: type of paper from the province of Echizen, ideal for prints.

IKEBANA: floral arrangement.

INU-HARIKO: papier-mâché dog.

JANOME-GASA: parasol with "snake's eye" motif.

JINGASA: flat helmet worn as armour.

KABUKI: popular citizen's theatre, originating from the 17th century.

KAISHI: "pocket paper"; an almost square paper format, used in calligraphy.

KAMI or SHI: paper.

KAMI: shinto divinity.

KAMIKO: paper clothing.

KAMI-SUKI: "rearing of paper".

KANA: Japanese syllabaries invented in the 8th and 9th centuries; originally used mainly by women to write poems and novels.

KARA-KAMI: originally "Chinese paper", based on continental models, and later, stencilled paper for covering sliding partitions.

KASANE-NO-IROME: overlapping of colours.

KATA-GAMI: stencil for printing fabrics.

KATA-SHIRO: shinto object used in incantations.

KIHADA: plant used in dyeing to produce a yellow colour.

KIRI-KAMI: cutout paper.

KONNYAKU: mucilaginous substance taken from arum.

KOZO: *broussonetia kajinoki*, a variety of mulberry tree used in the manufacture of paper.

MAIKO: Geisha novice.

MANEKI-NEKO: "cat calling" upon the wealth of tradesmen.

MAYUGAMI: kind of paper used for transcribing the syllabaries used in women's poetry.

MINO-GAMI: paper from the Gifu region.

MITSUMATA: *edgeworthia papyrifera*, a plant specific to Japan, used in the manufacture of paper.

MIZUHIKI: paper string for ceremonial wrapping.
MURASAKI: plant used in dyeing to produce a violet colour.
NADE-NINGYO: paper effigy used to ward off illness.
NAGASHI-BINA: paper doll thrown into the current to carry away the demons of illness.
NAGASHI-ZUKI: technique of "floating the fibres" on a sieve during paper making.
NERI or NORI: a mucilaginous substance used in paper making.
NO: chivalrous theatre of the ruling class developed in the 15th century.
NORI-UTSUGI: plant from which mucilage is extracted for paper making.
NOSHI: votive symbol indispensable to all ceremonial wrapping.
ODAWARA-JOCHIN: sleeve lantern originally made in the Odawara region.
OGI: ceremonial fan.
O-MIKUJI: oracle drawn and read at shinto shrines.
ORI-GAMI: the art of folding paper.
ORI-GATA: a folded shape.
ORI-KAMI: folded paper.
ORI-KATA: way of folding.
SAKAKI: shinto sacred tree.
SAKE: alcoholic drink made from rice.
SEMMEN: cutout in the shape of a fan, used in calligraphy.
SENSU: folding fan.
SHI or KAMI: paper.
SHIFU: weaving of paper threads.
SHIKISHI: "pretty sheet" with an almost square paper format, used for calligraphy.
SHIMENAWA: taboo rope in the shinto religion.
SHINTO: "Way of the Gods"; an exclusively Japanese religion venerating the gods of nature.
SHOGUN: originally "generalissimo at war with the Barbarians" before becoming the civil and military ruler of Japan in 1192, with the Emperor only retaining his role as religious head.
SHOJI: window hung with paper.
SUKI-ZOME: dyeing of fibres before the paper pulp is made.
SUMO: martial art representing the mythical combat of the shinto gods.
SURUGA-HANSHI: half-format paper from the prefecture of Shizuoka.
TAKO: kite.
TANZAKU: rectangular paper format for calligraphy.
TATAMI: mat of pressed straw.
TENGUCHO-SHI: very thin paper from the Kochi region (Tosa).
TOKONOMA: alcove of honour in the reception room of a home.
TORINOKO: kind of flecked paper resembling a quail's egg.
TORO: religious lantern.
TORORO-AOI: plant from which the mucilage used in paper making is obtained.
TOSA-WASHI: paper from the Kochi region.
TSUITATE: screen made from a single panel resting on feet.
TSUKE-ZOME: dyeing of sheets of already made-up paper.
TSUTSUMI: traditional wrapping generally consisting of paper string (mizuhiki) and noshi.
UCHIWA: flat fan.
UKIYO-E: print representing the "floating world".
WA-GASA: Japanese parasol.
WASHI: Japanese paper.
YAMABUSHI: Buddhist sect based on asceticism, having many characteristics in common with the shinto religion.
YO-SHI: Western paper.
YOSHINO-GAMI: paper from the Yoshino region.
YUZEN: painting directly onto silk.
ZEN: Buddhist sect giving great importance to meditation and linked to the development of many Japanese arts.

Acknowledgements

Kobo workshop in Ogawa, Karacho workshop in Kyoto, Sakaide workshop in Gifu, Tako-hachi workshop in Shizuoka, Tanaka workshop in Ogawa, Uno workshop in Kochi, Yamazen workshop in Kyoto, Akira and Takashi Buseki, Maryse Bonnaud, Masahiro Chatani, Mr and Mrs Enatsu, Ennosuke Ichikawa III, Mr and Mrs Fukumoto, Toshimichi Hiroi, Susumu Hirose, Hisao Honda, AkioHosokawa, Shozo Iida, Atsuko and Junko Inobe, Toshio Inoue, Shinichiro Ishii, Mr Iwai, Manabu and Liliko Iwasaki, Bernard Jeannel, Marc Peter Keane, Ryo and Hiromi Kinoshita, Taki Kishi, Yoshio Kitayama, Kazuo Kobayashi, Takashi and Chie Kuroda, the Kurodani paper-making centre, Junko Kusunoki, Jiko Kyodo, Jan and Hélène Lühl, Yoshimi and Noriko Maruyama, Setsuko Masuda, Hiroshi Matsuyama, Tokyo Kite Museum, Kochi Tosa-washi Museum, Tokyo Paper Museum, Meguro Museum of Art in Tokyo, Issey Miyake, Tokuko Miyamoto, Mr. Miyawaki, Kumiko Mizoguchi, Yoshihide Momotani, Shinichi and Reiko Nadai, Maki Nakagawa, Shoichi Nasegawa, Morio Nishio, Izumi Oshima, the Tokyo Origami-kaikan Centre, the prefecture of Kochi, Unno Sadaji, Kenjiro Sakamoto, Yoshitaka Sasai, Kenichi Senda, Shigeo Shinjo, Kyoto Shozan Company, Eiji Sugimoto, Masu Suzuki, Isako Tamura, Koji Tashiro, Osafu Tazawa, Hideaki Tomooka, Fumiko Tonomura, Ume Tsuda, the maiko Tsunemara, Seizo Tsuzura, Toyoaki Uno, Midori Yanai, Noriko Yasue, Kumi Yokomori, Takao Yoshida of the Kyoto Handycraft Centre, Toshihuki Yoshikawa, Sachio Yoshioka, Motozo Yoshizaki, Akira Yoshizawa, Chie Yuhara.

By the same author

Temples et sanctuaires au Japon, Édition du Moniteur, Paris, 1980.

Kimono, art traditionnel du Japon, Édita/La Bibliothèque des Arts, Lausanne, 1983.

Regards sur la femme japonaise in collaboration with Natacha Hochman, Éditions du Perron, Liège/Hatier, Paris, 1985.

La vie et l'œuvre de Léonard Tsuguharu Foujita in collaboration with Sylvie Buisson, A.C.R. Édition, Paris, 1987.

Le chat vu par les peintres, Inde, Corée, Chine, Japon, Édita S.A., Lausanne, 1988.

Manuel pratique d'origami, Édition Arted, Paris, 1988.

Architectures sacrées du Japon, A.C.R. Édition, Paris, 1989.

Papiers pliés, J'ai Lu, Paris, 1989.